D1476885

THE ZONE SYSTEM CRAFT BOOK

A COMPREHENSIVE GUIDE TO THE ZONE SYSTEM
OF EXPOSURE AND DEVELOPMENT

John Charles Woods

WCB Brown &
Benchmark

Book Team

Developmental Editor *Susan J. McCormick*
Production Coordinator *Karen Baumann-Nickolas*

A Division of Wm. C. Brown Communications, Inc.

Vice President and General Manager *Thomas E. Doran*
Executive Managing Editor *Ed Bartell*
Executive Editor *Edgar J. Laube*
Director of Marketing *Kathy Law Laube*
National Sales Manager *Eric Ziegler*
Marketing Manager *Pamela Cooper*
Advertising Manager *Jodi Rymer*
Managing Editor, Production *Colleen A. Yonda*
Manager of Visuals and Design *Faye M. Schilling*

Production Editorial Manager *Vickie Putman Caughron*
Publishing Services Manager *Karen J. Slaght*
Permissions/Records Manager *Connie Allendorf*

Wm. C. Brown Communications, Inc.

Chairman Emeritus *Wm. C. Brown*
Chairman and Chief Executive Officer *Mark C. Falb*
President and Chief Operating Officer *G. Franklin Lewis*
Corporate Vice President, Operations *Beverly Kolz*
Corporate Vice President, President of WCB Manufacturing *Roger Meyer*

Cover and interior design by Lesiak/Crampton Design Inc

Cover photo "Succulent Santa Barbara, California (1978)" by John Charles Woods. The Zone System allows the photographer full creative control of the gray tones in a photograph. The tonal relationships are easily predictable before the film is exposed, and the scene can be interpreted to suit personal, creative needs.

Copyedited by Pat Stevens

Some of the technical procedures included in this text may be hazardous if materials are handled improperly or if procedures are conducted incorrectly. Safety precautions are necessary when you are working with chemicals, or for any procedures that generally require caution. Your school may have set regulations regarding safety procedures that your instructor will explain to you. Should you have any problems with materials or procedures, please ask your instructor for help.

Copyright © 1993 by Wm. C. Brown Communications, Inc. All rights reserved

Library of Congress Catalog Card Number: 91-75900

ISBN 0-697-13190-4

No part of this publication may be reproduced, stored in a retrieval system, or transmitted, in any form or by any means, electronic, mechanical, photocopying, recording, or otherwise, without the prior written permission of the publisher.

Printed in the United States of America by Wm. C. Brown Communications, Inc., 2460 Kerper Boulevard, Dubuque, IA 52001

10 9 8 7 6 5 4 3 2 1

THE ZONE SYSTEM CRAFT BOOK

John Charles Woods

This book is dedicated to David and Klara Woods, who made unusual choices in children. I am grateful for this.

CONTENTS

PREFACE

No system of exposure and development is more famous or more shrouded in myth than the Zone System. Historically, comprehensive texts on the subject have frightened students due to their technicality. The simplified versions have either neglected vital information, forgotten to list the system's limitations, or disguised the system in an effort to avoid the stigma of technicality.

This text divides concept and procedure suggesting that concepts need not be approached technically and that technical information need not be eliminated for simplification.

Technical procedure is separated from the ideas of the main text and the student is referred to technical chapters that are used when needed. This provides an atmosphere for learning that is not cluttered by details but also makes available a concise reference source.

Using non-technical language, the general text is a primary, generic approach (in terms of specific films and developers) to exposure and development of black and white photographs and should not become dated.

Beginning with visualization as a creative tool, the text continues through light meter concepts, using the meter to make gray tones, manipulating these tones through development control, printing controls, and using the background of Zone System terminology for communication and problem solving.

Included are alternative processing methods for contrast reduction, such as the use of highly diluted developers to produce disproportionate development and the substitution of special films for extreme contrast increases.

Zone System myths and the basis for technical standards in film speed, light meter calibration, printing paper grades and other areas of photography are detailed.

It includes step-by-step testing procedures with specific goals that apply to testing most sensitized materials. The testing section offers a visual method for situations where sensitometry is not desired or not possible, and a simplified approach to testing using the densitometer for higher precision. A basic course in applied sensitometry is also included with explanations of densitometer use, what densities are, and how they relate to the Zone System.

All chapters are referenced to technical sections where students can find detailed information about processes and realistic limitations of the system. Included are alternate methods of communicating photographic technique and peripheral information pertaining to exposure and development of black and white materials.

Chapters are summarized and each summary offers simple tests to clarify concepts introduced in each chapter. The films used in these tests may also be applied to the later, specific test information.

This is not a general photographic text and adheres closely to the methods and ideas of Zone System thinking and application. Students who desire a practical mastery of black and white photography may use this text to improve photographic control or as a first step toward an understanding of applied sensitometry.

A strong emphasis is placed on the individuality of the photographer and the validity of imaginative use of craft. The necesssity of personal choice in the selection of subject matter and the amount of technical control that should be applied to a photograph, is also stressed.

ACKNOWLEDGMENTS

Thanks to Larry Dean, Ross Hernandez, and Doug Kopinski for starting the project and their confidence in me. Carl Burden deserves a special medal for tolerating the tedious testing of some new methods and a shield to protect him from all the ideas that I bounced off him.

Barbara and Richard Chang made this book possible—she with her typing and computer skills and he with his insightful technical expertise and constant feedback about where to go next. Thanks to Kim D. May, the world champ for long term loans. The manuscript owes its computer birth to Greg Rager who made it a labor of friendship.

My special thanks to Lorraine Zielinski, Karen Baumann-Nickolas and my zinfandel friend Susan McCormick, for making my association with Brown & Benchmark so pleasant.

Margaret Dew and Jacqui Burke-Woods were always there with support, typing assistance and true friendship. I thank David Drake, Ron Miller, Rob Johnson, and Jerry Burchfield who taught me the meaning of "normal," special thanks to John Placko from Ilford and finally I thank C. Joseph Gough . . . who feeds me.

I used about 90% of the suggestions submitted to me by the reviewers and it made for a substantially better book. It proves that a *diversity* of opinions is essential to good education. Thanks to those whom I have not yet met.

David R. Allison—Northern Virginia Community College
Emmette Jackson—Sam Houston State University
Gregory T. Moore—Kent State University
William G. Muller—Hudson Valley Community College
Gary B. Pearson—Ricks College
Michael Peven—University of Arkansas
Kenneth D. Pirtle—Amarillo College

AUTHOR'S NOTE

This text assumes a basic understanding of camera operation and film processing techniques. Although some procedures are described, they may not be detailed enough for the absolute beginner.

The Zone System is understandable even with minimal photographic experience, but unless basic camera operations and processing procedures are understood, the system may be difficult to *use*.

Chapter 7, "The Monkey Wrench," is a reference chapter. It is somewhat technical in nature and it is designed to free the main text from the many details of the Zone System that sometimes overwhelm the beginner. Sections of the main text are footnoted with the MW symbol* and the reader may refer to chapter 7 for clarification of an idea or an explanation of a specific procedure. MW-P indicates a specific procedure for using special materials or processes. The chapter is also cross referenced to the main text and can be read as a strictly technical "potpourri" of photographic information.

The chapter on sensitometry is also moderately technical. It introduces the student to the use of the densitometer and the relationship of sensitometry to the Zone System. For some students it may be wise to refrain from reading this section until the general concepts of the Zone System can be used as reference points for the more technical approach to testing.

BRIEF DEFINITIONS OF SPECIAL ZONE SYSTEM TERMINOLOGY

BRIGHTNESS

This refers to the amount of light reflected by an object. White paint reflects more light and looks brighter than black velvet when both are viewed in the same light. Technically this word is used only when describing actual light sources but this text will use the broader, more common definition for simplicity's sake.

COMPACTION

Indicates a lessening of contrast in either the negative or print by moving the zone values closer together.

EXPANSION

A contrast increase that moves zone values farther apart.

FALL

This refers to how different brightnesses in the scene produce different gray tones. If a subject is a zone V tone, then any part of the scene that is brighter must *fall* on (look like) a lighter zone. Any part of the scene that is darker must *fall* on a darker zone. This is how one object looks when compared to another in terms of gray tones.

PLACE OR PLACEMENT

The process of making a gray tone using exposure controls. The deliberate recording of a subject on a specific gray tone. The sentence, "I will place that tree on zone V" translates as, "I want that tree to look like a zone V shade of gray in the print."

EXPOSURE ZONE OR ZONE VALUE

A visual measurement usually used to indicate one of a series of 10 gray tones in a photograph (see Figure 1.1). In an actual scene, it refers to an area that will be recorded as one of these 10 tones.

CHAPTER 1 Introduction and Overview

This book's presentation suggests that photographic technique is a vehicle for the creation of expressive photographs. It sets a priority of personal interpretation as the final goal of a photograph. It also implies the Zone System was designed as a special tool to assist the photographer in the creative process and not to produce the "perfect negative." The system is concerned with the basic concepts of how a scene can be translated into a photographic print. The system can be used with any type of photography and need not be difficult or complex. The text stresses that everyone's creative choices are valid and that with an understanding of technical concepts, self expression is possible through photography.

The late 1800s saw the first systematic approach to the modern science of photography through the experiments of Hurter and Driffield. They mathematically graphed the effect of exposure and development on the negative and print in an attempt to create a consistent way to manipulate the photographic image.

By the 1930s reliable light meters could be used to predict negative densities with accuracy, but the most efficient method of communicating this information was in strictly scientific terms. It was largely ignored by the working photographer who still preferred the trial and error method of determining exposure and development.

The final organization of the Zone System was completed in the 1940s by photographers Ansel Adams and Fred Archer while they were working at the Art Center School in Los Angeles. It grew from an understanding of the science of exposure and development, called sensitometry, and the need to teach this science in a creative context.

Long before this time, the precise reactions of films to exposure and development were well known. What was needed was a method to apply sensitometry to the creative process so non-scientists could understand it. This required taking numbers, densities, brightnesses, and other technical terms and reducing them to a simple, visual notation. This visual scale provided a reference you could point to and say "I want it to look like that" and then actually make it work.

Essentially, the Zone System explains how to make the gray tones in a black and white photograph do what we want. It shows how to mix exposure and development in the same way a painter mixes paints. It was out of this desire to personalize the "mixing" that the Zone System was created. The artistic decisions are made by the photographer and not left to machinery. This does not limit the use of modern technological advances in equipment, but it modifies the use of such equipment and gives the photographer a choice. The Zone System suggests creativity is the result of human decisions and practical technique. This philosophy is expressed by photographer Minor White who wrote, "The amateur who realizes he is a victim of his equipment and materials can discover in the Zone System a positive means of mastering his medium."

One of the greatest concerns of photographers is to develop a consistency of results that reduces the element of chance. Most approaches to this problem stress technical accuracy without addressing the problems of language and its ambiguities. The standardization of terms and the introduction of specific reference gray tones provides an environment for technical and visual consistency based on creative decisions.

A minimum of numbers and technical jargon will be used in the main text. The attempt is to broaden the audience that can understand and use photography. This is the science of photography expressed in non-scientific terms.

VISUALIZATION

Visualizing the print is the first vital concept in using the Zone System. This means imagining the way we want to translate the scene into the gray tones of a photograph. It can be used to record the scene as literally as possible or to depart dramatically from reality. The degree of departure is determined by the photographer, and it is important to understand that any degree of control is valid, even if the control is deliberately minimal. This is not an advocation of sloppy technique; it is more a recommendation for each worker to determine how far to carry the possibilities of technical control. Personalization of the photograph is the underlying goal of the system.

All aspects of the system are based on the artistic premise that the photographer should make some decision about how the photograph should look *before* the film is exposed. These decisions are the basis for the personalization of each photograph. Even if the technical ability of two photographers is the same, the way they decide to visualize the print may vary enormously.

Even with the most modern equipment and methods, many of the characteristics of the negative are determined by the film exposure and cannot easily be changed. In this sense visualization becomes an important aspect of technique because it sets the basic nature of all technical decisions.

The idea behind visualization is simple. We imagine the way we want a scene to look and then make it look that way. In reality, it requires practice and attention to become intuitive. Thinking in terms of photographic materials and their limits differs in difficulty depending upon the individual. Some visualization problems are technical and some are problems of interpretation. The different aspects of visualization are discussed in detail throughout the text.

THE GRAY SCALE

A black and white photograph is made up of gray tones. If we control these tones we control the nature of the photograph—both emotional and technical. In the average photograph the number of possible gray tones is so large it must be simplified so it can be discussed intelligently. Just as a piano keyboard cannot produce every possible musical note, we cannot control every possible gray tone. It is possible, however, to selectively control parts of the gray scale to produce the results we want. We generalize these tone areas into zones.

Figure 1.1 shows a continuous gray scale and the same scale divided into ten distinct gray tones from black to white. The scale symbolizes the simplified tonalities of a photograph. These tones are numbered and called zones or zone values. Each zone value is a specific shade of gray which does not change and is numbered 0–IX. The pure black of the photograph is always called zone value 0 and in this text zone value IX is always the whitest white the paper can produce. The zones are usually numbered using Roman numerals. This avoids confusion with the shutter speed, f-stop and exposure value numbers that are used in light meter and camera operation.

MW 1

This illustration should be carefully examined by the reader to clarify the gray scale concept and how it applies to an actual photograph. This is the first step in learning to visualize a print because we now have a consistent set of reference tones.

We distinguish between print *values* and negative *values* because the print value is a literal gray tone while any area of the negative can be printed to any tone by changing the exposure time given to the print. The negative zone values are relative to each other and the print values are absolute.

The division of the continuous gray scale into ten distinct values is one of convenience. Though it is practical to think in terms of specific shades of gray, a zone is really a small range of adjacent gray tones. There is some degree of tolerance in defining a print value since it represents a zone of grays. The divided gray scale is most easily represented as the midpoint of each area of tones (Figure 1.2).

A common misunderstanding occurs when students point at an object such as a building and ask, "What zone is that building?" In literal print value terms, it is any zone you decide it should be. Zones as literal tones do not exist in nature because a zone value is a *translation* of an object into a *chosen* gray tone in a print. Any object we photograph can be made any print value we want. This demonstrates the interpretive nature of the Zone System because each photographer decides what print value the building shall be.

To the camera, an object in a scene is just a brightness. It can make no decision as to the object's importance to our photograph or about what gray tone would properly represent that object. The Zone System generalizes these areas of brightness and calls them exposure zones. For example, a white wall in sunlight is a distinctly different brightness than the same wall in shade. Each general area can be called an exposure "zone" since it is really made up of many subtle brightnesses which produce the effect of one overall tone. As the Zone System gray scale generalizes the continuous gray scale of the print, the idea of exposure zones generalizes the continuous brightness range of the subject. This flexible approach to tone identification can simplify the visualization process but also has some drawbacks which will be discussed in later chapters.

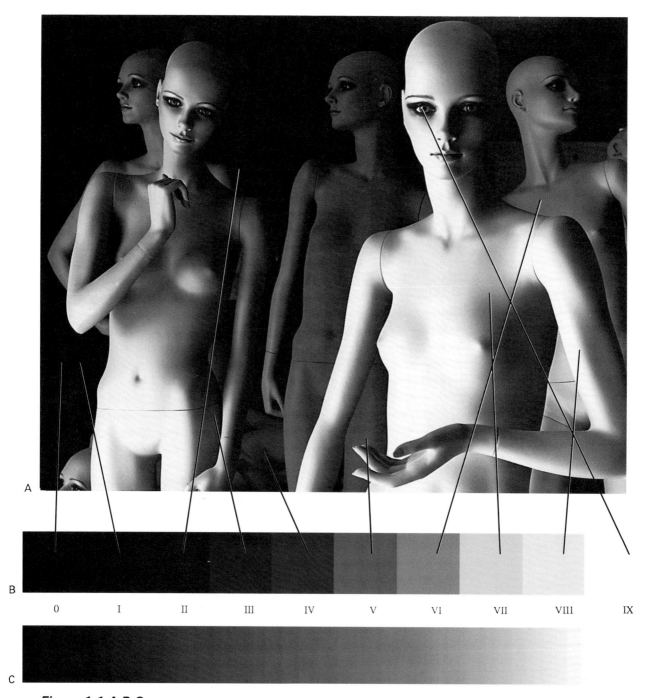

A

B

| 0 | I | II | III | IV | V | VI | VII | VIII | IX |

C

Figure 1.1 A,B,C   *The Zone System divides the continuous gray scale (C) into ten distinct gray tones (B) to aid visualization of the final photograph.*
   (A) shows these gray tones as they appear in a scene. Significant values include zone III, the lowest fully detailed tone, zone V, a medium gray tone, and zone VII, the lightest gray tone that retains full image detail.

Centerpoint

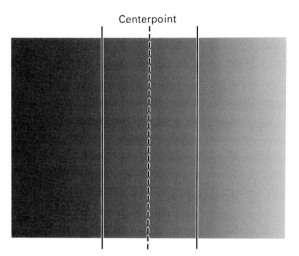

Figure 1.2 *Since it is a division of the continuous gray scale, a "zone" is really a subtle graduation of tones from dark to light. The center of this area of tones is used to represent the zone in the divided gray scale. The figure represents the medium tones of the continuous scale, approximately a zone V value.*

The distinction between exposure zones and print values is subtle, but it is necessary to use different terminology when describing the subject, the negative, and the print.

These terms link the subject with how it records on the film and how it looks on the print. When we talk of a tree being on zone V we mean that it is either zone value V on the print or we have exposed the film with the intention of making it zone V. For easy reference remember that zone 0 equals zero light. The higher the zone number the lighter the gray tone.

Many students have trouble translating the brightnesses of the subject to the densities[1] of the negative and then back to the print. To avoid confusion, the text will discuss the way the final print will look when the negative is made using Zone System methods. This approach directly relates the brightness of the subject to the lightness of the gray tone. Discussion of the densities of the negative will be delayed until the basic concepts of the Zone System are understood.

If we want something lighter (higher) on the zone scale, we add either more light or more development. If we want to make something darker we must reduce exposure or development. *Different parts of the gray scale are affected depending upon whether we change the exposure or the development but the concept is the same.*

Just as written music is not the actual music that is played, the negative value is not the actual tone that is seen in the print. The sheet music is the *intention* of the note to be played and the negative value is the *intention* of the tone to be printed. In this subtle way the word "zone" differs from the words "tone" or "value" since it implies not only the physical tone in the print but also the artistic decision made by the photographer. As we might play a note differently than a musical score suggests, so can we print a negative value differently to fulfill our personal needs.

---

[1] The term *density* refers to the ability of the negative to block different amounts of light. The greater the density the less light will pass through it; i.e., sunglasses have greater density than normal glass and pass less light.

LIGHT METERS

The exposure that film receives can be determined by guessing, by experience, or by the use of a light measuring device—a light meter. A light meter is a device that relates film sensitivity to the brightnesses of the actual scene. For the student it avoids guesswork in determining exposures. For the more advanced photographer, it supplements experience to provide precise control of the photograph. A description of how light meters work is necessary to understand their use with the Zone System.

Light meters measure light; they do not necessarily give us the "correct" exposures. If your use of the light meter gives you the results you want then the exposures it gives you are correct. Your expectations may change as your experience grows, and your personal definition of correct exposure will also change. Some methods of using a light meter assume that only one exposure can render a scene accurately. The Zone System is based on the principle that the correct exposure is a matter of personal, creative expectations and that a light meter is a tool to use for information.

The type of light meter most commonly used in photography is the reflected light meter. This tool measures the light that is reflected from the subject, the light that we see and that forms the photographic image. The other type of meter that is commonly used is the incident meter. It measures the light falling on the subject. The incident meter does not measure the light reflected from the subject and is not easily applied to the Zone System. The incident meter and its use will be discussed briefly in Chapter 4.

Reflected Light Meters

Reflected light meters all function in the same basic way. They are essentially very simple machines. Films are rated according to their sensitivity to light, and light meters are designed to work according to these ratings. They provide exposure recommendations of varied accuracy depending upon their quality. The word recommendation is used since the variations of lighting conditions are so complex. No meter or metering system can encompass every possible picture taking situation. For this reason many different measuring systems have been developed to try to find a way to give consistently good results in a variety of situations.

Several examples of light meter usage are shown in Figure 1.3 A, B, C, and D. In each case the area of the scene that is measured by the meter is indicated. Some examples show the use of handheld light meters and some represent actual in-camera light measuring systems. In each case the reflected light is measured, even though the part of the scene that is measured may differ with each system. Light meters and metering systems measure the objects they see and suggest these objects should be rendered as a medium gray tone equal to the value we call zone V. This specific gray tone is the same as the 18% gray card which can be found at the end of this text. If the meter sees many different brightnesses in a scene it will integrate these brightnesses and try to record the average brightness as a zone V value.

 MW 2   If we granted a reflected light meter the ability to talk, its vocabulary would be limited to a single sentence. The sentence would never vary and its simplicity shows the basic limitations of these devices. The sentence

would be, "Whatever I see (measure), I will recommend an exposure to make that thing look like a zone V value." This is tone V on the zone scale in Figure 1.1.

In Figure 1.3 A, a handheld *spot* meter measures a very small part of the scene. The recommended exposure would record that part of the scene as zone value V. Any scene area can be measured.

The term "spot metering" means measuring only very small areas of the scene. It usually refers to a reading area of approximately 10 degrees or less. This example measures a 1-degree area.

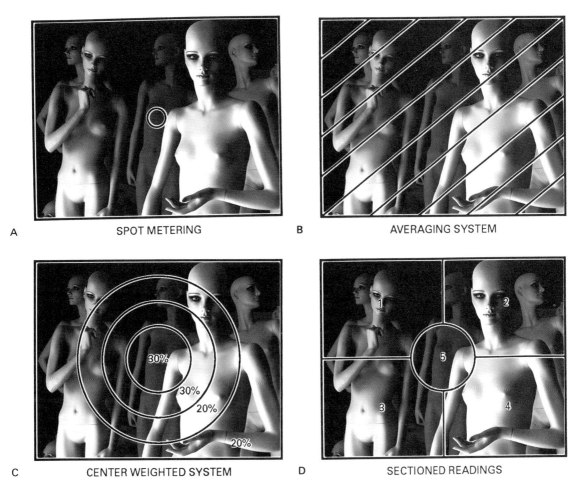

A   SPOT METERING   B   AVERAGING SYSTEM

C   CENTER WEIGHTED SYSTEM   D   SECTIONED READINGS

Figure 1.3 A,B,C,D   *These figures represent the areas of a scene measured by various metering methods. They do not show the effect of the methods, only the parts of the scene that are measured. All of the systems measure reflected light only.*

Figure A illustrates the use of a spot meter. Spot metering may be done with a handheld meter or a in-camera system offering a spot meter option. The figure shows a 1-degree measuring area.

Figure B shows an "averaging" method of light meter use. The entire scene area is measured, usually with a wide field meter. Several spot meter readings of different areas can be used to "average" the scene if they are made from the proper scene areas.

Figure C demonstrates how a "center weighted" system provides disproportionate light readings. The percentage numbers indicate the amount of the total light that is measured from the scene areas.

Figure D shows a system that divides into sections for measurement. Different systems integrate the readings in different proportions, and the size and shape of the sections may differ.

In Figure 1.3 B, the entire scene is measured and the total of the brightnesses is averaged to a zone V tone. The areas that are brighter than this average will be lighter than zone V; the areas that are darker will be rendered darker than zone V. This is called "averaging" and can be done with the in-camera meter or with a handheld meter.

In Figure 1.3 C, the meter takes most of its information from the center of the frame and about 30–40% from the rest of the scene. These readings are integrated in different proportions. This is called a center-weighted system.

In Figure 1.3 D, several small areas are read and then integrated. Some readings are favored more than others. Some in-camera systems work in this manner.

It appears some systems might perform better or worse depending upon the situation, and this is true. The cohesive demonstration of how all meters work the same way occurs when we place an evenly lit, single-toned subject, like a large white card, in front of each meter. Each meter system would give an exposure that would place it on zone V. In every system it is as if the photographer made light measurements from different parts of the scene and integrated them as needed. The meter gave the same information every time but the total number of readings and location of the readings differed. It is important to realize that for each reading, the meter provided the same exposure information.

If we scan a scene making selective measurements, any area of the subject, the brightest or darkest object in the scene, can be rendered a zone value V depending upon where the measurement is made.

Each system performs a useful function depending on its priorities. *All* systems can be accurate depending upon situation and use. The single thing that no light meter can do is decide which areas of the photograph are important to *you*. The most that is possible is for the system's designer to second-guess the common human element. If enough people make enough photographs in similar ways, we can itemize these factors and design a system that works most of the time. Each system's design is attempting to do this.

All these metering systems lack the discrimination to determine which part of the scene is significant. The Zone System is based upon the photographer selecting the significant areas of the picture. This is the difference between the photographer who gets what is desired and one who accepts what a machine decides is correct.

Any system can be used creatively provided you learn it, work within its limits, and apply it to your personal criteria. With the Zone System the light meter is used on its most simplistic level. It requires more participation from the photographer and more decision making, but it is actually a more creative use of the information the meter provides. It also leads to a fuller understanding of the thinking behind all metering systems.

CHAPTER 1 SUMMARY

Visualization means imagining the final print before the film is exposed and deciding how we want it to look. The Zone System is based on each photographer's personal interpretation of a scene.

The continuous gray scale of the photograph is divided in ten distinct gray tones which symbolize subject brightnesses. The tones are numbered and called exposure zones or zone values. The extremes of this zone scale are pure black, zone 0, and pure white zone IX. Using a standardized gray scale helps to provide technical and visual consistency.

All reflected type light meters are designed to tell us how to make a middle gray tone. If a light meter could talk it would always say, "Whatever I see, I will tell you an exposure to make it look like a zone V tone."

Any area of the subject can be recorded as zone V. This can be the brightest or darkest object in the scene depending upon where the measurement is made.

TEST

If any of the ideas in Chapter 1 are unclear, this simple test will demonstrate the relationship of light meters to recording gray tones.

Using the manufacturer's film speed, make several exposures of subjects of different brightnesses. I recommend at least one subject be a light colored object in sunlight and another subject, in a separate exposure, a dark object in shade. This provides extreme cases. In every exposure the metered area will produce the same tone.

Be careful that the light meter readings are made of evenly lit, single-toned objects. It may be necessary to move in close to measure objects with in-camera meters. Only the area measured will record as zone V. Other areas will record differently unless they are the same brightness as the measured object. Shutter variations can cause erratic results. Even slight variations in subject lighting will show up, so look for overall tonal effects when judging prints.

Develop all negatives for the same time. If all negatives are printed on the same grade of paper (I recommend grade #2) at the same exposure and developed together, the measured objects will always be the same gray tone.

Save these negatives for future reference and record this data: Film type and speed, developer type, temperature, time, and dilution used.

If you do not desire a negative, Polaroid films may be used for this test. If the tests are conducted outdoors, be certain to keep film at an even temperature for processing.

Bodie, California, 1975 *A wide field meter was brought close to the weathered wood area in the lower right of the scene. The recommended exposure was used and this general area was automatically placed on zone V. The film was developed normally.*

CHAPTER 2 Making Gray Tones

Although there are virtually an unlimited number of gray tones possible in a black and white print, we will concern ourselves with the ten full tones shown in Figure 1.1. Much finer graduations of the scale are possible but the ten tones are more than sufficient for visualizing a print.

We work with ten zones for two main reasons: (1) they correspond to the full f-stop and shutter speed increments of most cameras, and (2) if there are too many tones they are difficult to remember. This is called the Zone System because it generalizes tones, not because it is designed to produce scientifically perfect negatives.

As shown in Chapter 1, the reflected light meter tells us how to make zone V, tone #5 on the gray scale. The reason for choosing this particular tone is somewhat arbitrary and is based on this kind of thinking:

- The meter is a simple measuring device and can only tell us how to make one tone directly.
- If it gave us exposures that made everything pure black (zone 0), it would be useless. We would not need to expose the film at all.
- Conversely, if it told us how to make everything pure white (zone IX), it would be equally useless.

The rationale was to split the difference and select a medium gray (zone V) as a basis for the measurements. The reason for using a gray tone of 18% reflectance is discussed in Chapter 6. For our purposes this specific tone is the basis for all exposure determination.

Knowing our light meter always tells us how to make this zone V shade of gray, we can use this information to produce other tones in the photograph.

If we want an object to be some other tone than zone V we must give some other exposure than what the meter indicates. To make an object darker, we must take away light (decrease exposure) to the film. To make it lighter, we add light (increase exposure) to the film. Our camera controls are usually designed to change our exposure in specific increments. The shutter speeds on most cameras either double or halve our exposure, while every full f-stop (lens opening) change does precisely the same.

Each tone on our gray scale is the result of changing our exposure from what the light meter indicates. If we give precisely twice the light our meter indicates we have made our object record as zone VI. If we halve the exposure our meter indicates, we have made our object one full tone darker than zone V, or zone IV.

MW 3   These changes in tone will vary if the development time of the negative changes, so all of the tone relationships we shall discuss in this chapter will be based on developing the film to a *normal degree of contrast*. The definition of normal development is covered in Chapter 3.

Figure 2.1 A, 2.1 B and 2.1 C show how much change occurs when the exposure is varied by cutting it in half or doubling it. All negatives in these figures were developed normally.

By knowing the full f-stop and shutter speed increments on our camera either double or halve the exposure, we can use the light meter to tell us not only that one object is lighter or darker than another object, but also by how much. It does this in the terms of our camera controls and we can use these controls to make gray tones. Every time we double our exposure we move everything in our scene upward on the gray scale one zone. When we halve the exposure we move all tones downward one zone. If we do not double or halve the exposure when we change it, we produce tones that fall in between the full zones.

ZONE VALUE RELATIONSHIPS

The key to using the Zone System is in selecting which zone is personally correct for the subject. Light meters cannot decide which part of the scene is significant. If an object in a scene is consciously exposed to be a certain zone, we say it has been "placed" on an exposure zone. This is a deliberate act implying definite decisions. We choose to "place" an object based on many factors including the size of the object, the context of the rest of the scene, the amount of detail desired and many other factors. We select a significant part of our scene, decide what gray tone we want it to be, and make an exposure that will render it that zone. Any other part of our scene that is equally bright will record as the same zone as the one that is "placed".

Figure 2.1 A

Changes in zone values can be compared in each photograph. All negatives were developed normally and printed at the same printing exposure time.

In Figure 2.1 A the central shadow area was measured and the recommended exposure was used.

A

Figure 2.1 B

Changes in zone values can be compared in each photograph. All negatives were developed normally and printed at the same printing exposure time.

In Figure 2.1 B the recommended exposure was reduced (underexposed) by 1 full f-stop which moved all of the values down the scale 1 full zone value.

B

Figure 2.1 C

Changes in zone values can be compared in each photograph. All negatives were developed normally and printed at the same printing exposure time.

In Figure 2.1 C the exposure was again decreased by 1 full f-stop (2 stops underexposed from Figure 2.1 A) and all the values moved down another zone. The areas of very dark values may give the illusion of greater contrast due to their large size. Cutting a hole in a piece of paper and viewing small areas of the reproduction through it may assist you in assessing the tone changes.

C

Objects that are brighter will record lighter than the placed object; darker objects will record on a lower zone. The parts of the scene that are not placed are said to *fall* on the scale of zones. This does not mean these values are unknown, just that they are relative to one key area that has been deliberately "placed" on a zone.

In Figure 2.2 A, the light was measured from the indicated area and the recommended exposure was used without modification. As predicted, the measured part of the wall was rendered as zone V. Since the shadowed part of the wall reflected less light it is recorded as a lower zone. Using the light meter we can determine, before exposing the film, just how much darker the shadowed wall is than the white wall. When we measure the difference in terms of the camera controls we can predict the tonal relationship between them.

Figure 2.2 B shows that when the reading is made from the darker area of the wall, that area is recorded as zone V. By comparing the two recommended exposures we can see the darker area reflects about three f-stops less light than the light section of the wall. This brightness difference tells the difference in zones. Three f-stops difference means three zones difference. If the lighter part of the white wall is placed on zone V by measuring it and using the recommended exposure, the shadowed wall must fall on zone II. It is three f-stops darker and each f-stop difference equals one zone difference. If the *shadowed* wall is placed on zone V then the light wall must fall on zone VIII. Although the exposure is different the relationship of the brightness and the zones is the same.

This is the relationship that occurs when the film is developed "normally" and printed on a "normal" grade of photographic paper. Both of these norms are defined later in the text. For now, a simple definition of normal development is what the manufacturer recommends, and a normal paper is one designated as a contrast grade #2.

Since we know the relationship of the objects in the scene, we can use either of the measurements to control the tones. We could, for instance, measure the lighter part of the wall and place it directly on zone VIII by giving the film three full f-stops *more* exposure than the meter recommends. The meter tells us how to make zone V and we know that for every full f-stop more exposure we give the film we move the gray tone up one step on the gray scale. Three steps up from zone V is zone VIII. We also know the shadowed wall is three f-stops darker than the light wall and must fall three zones lower, on zone V.

If we choose to make the shadowed wall record as zone III, the lighter wall must fall on zone VI being three f-stops brighter. The relationship of the zones does not change, only the literal zones that are recorded. We can make one area of the scene precisely the gray tone we want and also predict the gray tones of other areas of the picture with great accuracy.

Let us examine another scene in Figure 2.3. The numbers in the figure are the f-stops recommended by a selective reading of that area. For convenience, the shutter speed recommended is the same in each case. Specific areas have been selected for readings in order to ease the process of visualizing zone relationships.

The meter recommends f/16 as the zone V exposure for the sky, f/8 for the lighter areas of the concrete, f/5.6 for the shadowed concrete and f/2.8 for the extreme top of the bridge. If the shadowed concrete is metered and placed on zone V all of the relative zone values can be predicted for each subject area. The lighter concrete reading one f-stop brighter falls on zone VI. The sky records three zones higher because it is three f-stops brighter

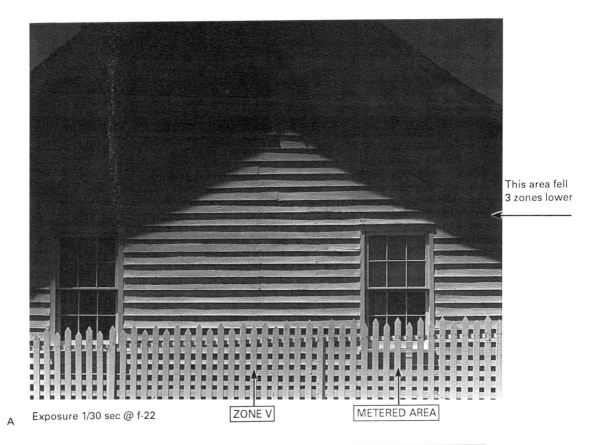

This area fell
3 zones lower

A   Exposure 1/30 sec @ f-22

ZONE V   METERED AREA

ZONE V

METERED AREA

This area fell
3 zones higher

B   Exposure 1/30 sec @ f-8

Figure 2.2 A,B   *In Figure 2.2 A the white paint in sunlight was measured, placed on zone V, and an exposure combination (f-stop and shutter speed) is noted. By comparing the first exposure to a zone V placement reading made from the paint in shade (Figure B), the difference in f-stops can be found. In this case about three f-stops difference is measured. The difference in f-stops tells us the difference in zone values with normal development.*

than the shadowed concrete. The top of the bridge is two f-stops darker than the shadowed concrete and falls on zone III. We could use any one of these readings to determine the exposure and the other zone values would be known. *As we change exposure all values move up and down the gray scale and they move in unison.*

MW 4

Some photographers use a Wratten #90 filter to assist the visualization process. The scene is viewed through this amber colored filter which neutralizes the colors to approximate the way the film would record it. Adjacent colors may look different to the eye but record as the same gray tone causing tone mergers. The filter helps avoid this problem.

I recommend using the #90 (also called a viewing filter) if you have difficulty visualizing the gray tones of the photograph; however, the filter approximates the film's response at normal development only and cannot show the effect of increasing or decreasing contrast for creative work.

EXPOSURE VALUES

Many light meters do not read in shutter speeds and f-stops directly. Some give whole numbers which are transferred to a separate meter dial which converts them to f-stop/shutter speed combinations. These numbers are called exposure values, or EV's (see Figure 2.4). Each number represents a full f-stop change in the brightness of the scene. Number 1 represents 1/2 the brightness of number 2; number 3 indicates twice the brightness of number 2, and so on. With these numbers the relative brightnesses of a scene are easily compared, which makes this type of meter ideal for Zone System use. In Figure 2.5 the EV numbers have been substituted for the f-stop readings for the scene. They do not represent zones but they tell us the brightness difference between objects. If the EV number read from the object is transferred to the meter dial, the exposure recommended would place that brightness on zone V. Like direct f-stop readings the EV numbers tell how many zones exist in the scene, one zone difference for every EV number. Remember these are not zone numbers; they are numbers that tell us relative brightnesses. An object may read EV 12, and we may place it on any zone we choose by modifying the recommended exposure.

Much confusion occurs with the numbers used in the Zone System. To the normal f-stop and shutter speed numbers, we add EV numbers and zone numbers. I urge the reader to consider that this confusion usually concerns the *operation of the equipment* and not the Zone System itself. The concepts of the Zone System do not involve any numbers except 0–9 (in Roman numerals 0–IX). All of the ideas can be understood without complex numbering.

Camera operation requires some facility with lens openings and shutter speeds, and transferring EV readings to the meter dial and then to the camera, can lead to mistakes. If you are confused about any of these numbers, review them before continuing.

Some cameras have EV numbers that can be directly set on the camera. They may be used to lock the shutter speed and f-stops together so that equivalent exposures can be made rapidly. Some older meters read in numbers that are *not* EV's and should be checked by comparison to a known meter.

We now have a simple method of selecting one area of a scene, measuring the light reflected from that area, and determining an exposure to place it on a zone of our choice. We can also predict how other areas of the scene will look in relation to the placed value. The light meter is used as

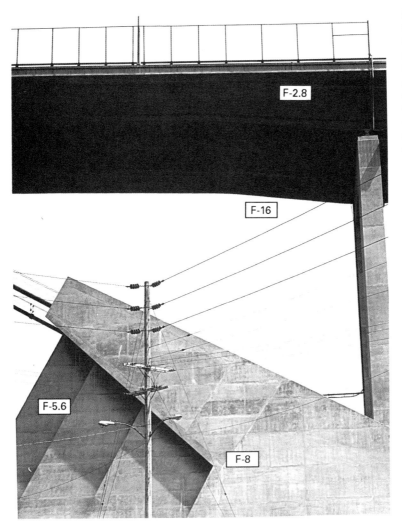

F-2.8

F-16

F-5.6

F-8

Figure 2.3 *F-stop readings from the scene areas are shown. If the negative is developed normally, the print values can be accurately predicted by comparing the brightness differences as measured in f-stops. A one f-stop difference equals a one zone difference. Any of the readings could be used to determine the exposure if the value is placed properly.*

Figure 2.4 *This light meter reads in exposure value numbers (EV's). The EV number measured from the scene is manually located opposite the triangular mark on the dial and exposure combinations for a zone V placement can be determined.*

Figure 2.5 *Exposure value numbers have been substituted for the f-stops in Figure 2.3. The EV's indicate the relative brightness of scene areas but they do not represent zone placements. Calculating zone differences is usually faster and easier using EV's.*

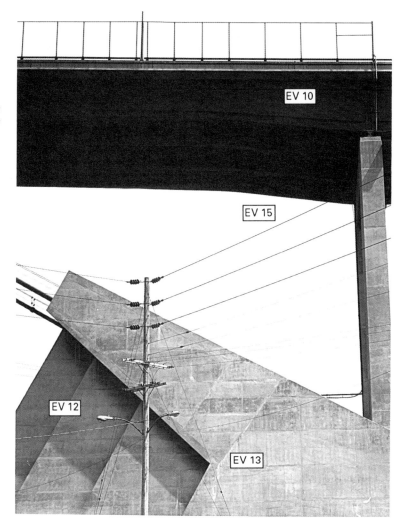

a measuring device and not as a machine that gives us "correct" exposures.

Until now we have dealt with the tonal relationships as they appear when the film is developed normally. The next chapter discusses development and how it can be used to alter zone relationships to suit our creative needs.

CHAPTER 2 SUMMARY

We can place any subject brightness on the gray scale by doing what the light meter tells us or by modifying the information. If we give less light than the meter indicates we move the subject toward the darker end of the zone scale. If we give more light we move the subject toward the lighter end of the zone scale. If we *double* the exposure all values move up precisely *one* full zone. If the exposure is cut in *half* all values move down precisely *one* full zone. Each full f-stop or shutter speed change will alter the exposure by precisely one full zone. All values move up or down in unison when exposure is changed.

We can measure any area of a scene and place it on the zone we select. All other subject areas can also be measured and their position on the zone scale predicted. If they are brighter than the placed object they will record as lighter tones; if they are darker they will record as darker tones. For each full f-stop difference that is measured, a one full zone difference will be recorded if the film is developed to a *normal degree of contrast.*

TEST

If the concepts of placing values on the zone scale or of predicting zone relationships by using the light meter are unclear, the following test will provide a practical demonstration of these ideas.

At the manufacturer's recommended film speed make a series of five different exposures of a sunlit outdoor scene. Determine the exposure by metering a subject area and placing it on a specific zone. Try starting with a shadow area or dark object and place it on what you consider the appropriate zone. Measure at least one other object in the scene that is noticeably brighter and note the difference in f-stops between it and the object that has been placed on a zone. Try to find an object that is no more than three or four f-stops brighter. The readings should tell you where the brighter object falls on the zone scale. One f-stop difference equals one zone difference *with normal development.*

Expose the film as follows:

Exposure #1   as determined by adjusting reading for your personal zone placement

Exposure #2   One full f-stop *less* than exposure #1

Exposure #3   Two full f-stops *less* than exposure #1

Exposure #4   One full f-stop *more* than exposure #1

Exposure #5   Two full f-stops *more* than exposure #1

Process the film as you normally do and dry. In each case the zone relationships will not change. All zones move up or down the scale in unison. Do not expect the scale to match the Zone System scale. We have not adjusted the processing to fine-tune it yet.

Record all exposure data as in Chapter 1 Test but add a description of which subject area was placed, and on what zone. Also note the other object measured and on what zone it should fall. *SAVE ALL NEGATIVES, they may be used for more specific tests later.* A sample of the notes for this test might read as follows:

Placed subject area—Wall placed on *zone III* by measuring and giving two f-stops *less* light than the meter indicates.

Measured subject area—Sky read 4 f-stops brighter than wall. The sky falls on *zone VII* if wall is placed on zone III.

Exposure given:

Exposure #1   f/8 @ 1/60 sec.   *These are sample*

Exposure #2   f/11 @ 1/60 sec.   *exposures only.*
                                             Your exposures
Exposure #3   f/16 @ 1/60 sec.   *may differ.*

Exposure #4   f/5.6 @ 1/60 sec.

Exposure #5   f/4 @ 1/60 sec.

If these negatives are all printed on the same grade of paper (grade #2) at the same print exposure, *the print values will move in unison with the changes in exposure given to the film.* Later these negatives can be used to fine tune the gray scale to your personal standards. Take care with your note taking to avoid inaccurate results.

If you do not desire a negative, Polaroid films can be used for this test and handled in the same manner as the ordinary films with the warning that they cannot reproduce as many zones as conventional films. Polaroid films are unsurpassed for immediate feedback and for group testing or demonstrations.

MW 5

Landscape—White Mountains, California 1977   *The base of the large tree at right was measured and the recommended exposure was decreased 2 full f-stops, placing the area on zone III. The sunlit bark measured a little over 4 f-stops higher and fell on zone VII 1/2. This relationship of tones seemed appropriate and normal development was selected. Small areas of the sunlit bark of the left tree measured more than 5 f-stops brighter than the placed area and were recorded as pure white (zone IX or higher). The print was made on grade #2 paper.*

CHAPTER 3 Moving Gray Tones

Before discussing the development process and how it helps build and move gray tones we must further define the zone scale using visual and verbal means. Aside from the actual tones that exposure produces there is another major consideration that must be addressed—the amount of image detail that is discernable in each zone. The scale that this text uses is one with a textured range of zone III to zone VII. This means that zone III is the lowest zone that shows *good* image detail and that zone VII is the highest one with *good* image detail. Zones outside these will record as the indicated zones but will have only tone with slight or no visible detail. (See Figure 3.1.)

This scale is the standard reference of this text and of most Zone System workers. This does not mean that it's correct in any abstract sense. It is merely a point of reference to which we may compare our results. The ten step scale with a textured range of zone III to zone VII is the product of technical and emotional decisions based on equipment designs, observation, and even highly subjective visual preferences. It is crucial to the photographer in terms of communicating knowledge of photographic craft. The ten step gray scale is not universally accepted but it is a common standard in a medium that cannot agree upon precisely what constitutes "normal" development. It can be argued that the textured range is zone II to zone VIII but the detail in these extreme zones is minimal. Much of these criteria are based on visual evaluations and selection of specific materials, but this textured range of zone III to zone VII is an excellent starting point and is used throughout this text.

MW 6

The two primary procedures in making a negative are exposure and development. We have seen in Chapter 1 that exposure changes move all zones up and down the scale together without changing their basic relationship. This relationship is based on *normal development* producing a one zone change for every f-stop difference that we measure.

Changes in development from normal alter zone relationships and the progression of zones is no longer considered normal. *When the film is developed for more than a normal time we get more than a one zone change for every f-stop difference that we measure. Less than normal development results in less than a one zone change for each measured f-stop difference.* These varied zone relationships are called contrast differences.

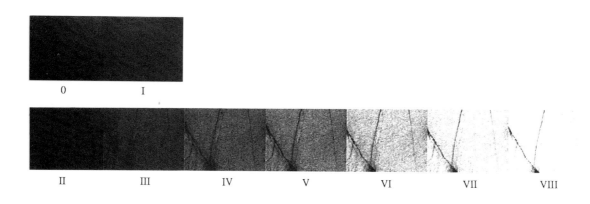

Figure 3.1 *The detailed gray scale for Zone System use. Zones II and VIII represent the maximum possible extremes of detail with zones III and VII being fully detailed. The film and paper combination determine the actual detailed scale that is practical. It is possible that zones II and VIII will show no detail with some materials. Note that even the extreme overexposure of a zone VIII placement cannot bring the deep rock cracks above a zone 0 value.*

MW 15   The word contrast is used to describe a variety of visual effects. For our purposes, increased contrast means moving zones apart; decreased contrast means moving zones closer together. Secondary definitions may be used later to describe other visual effects.

EFFECTS OF DEVELOPMENT ON CONTRAST

How and why zones move is more easily understood as we investigate how development works in forming an image. The more exposure an area of the film receives the greater its ability to move. When the film is developed, each zone is formed at a different rate. The lower the zone the more difficult it is to move. The higher the zone the more sensitive it is to development changes and it moves more easily.

Even the earliest experiments with film showed that the longer the development time, the higher the contrast of the negative. This means some zone values must be changing more than others. If all zones moved equally, the difference between them would not change and the effect would be the same as changing exposure. The fact that the high zones are more sensitive to development changes is one of the most useful creative tools we have.

MW 7   Because the lower zones move so little in the development process we can make large changes in development time without seriously affecting them. As the development time is *increased*, the higher zones move upward rapidly on the scale. A zone II will move very little, but a zone VI value may move up to a zone VI 1/2, and a zone VII may move up one full zone to zone VIII. The higher the zone the more it will move up the scale. To avoid confusion, a shortcut in terminology has been made for Zone System

use. When we increase development it is called a "plus" development; this causes an expansion of zones. A less than normal development is called a "minus" development, causing a compaction of zones. To indicate the amount of zone movement we add a number. A one zone upward movement is referred to as a *plus 1* development. A two zone upward movement is a *plus 2* development. Moving a zone down the scale one whole tone is a *minus 1*, two tones is a *minus 2* and so on.

For instance, in HC-110 developer dilution B (1+7), my normal development time for Kodak T-Max 400 sheet film is 7 1/2 minutes, a normal *plus 1* time is 9 minutes, and normal *plus 2* time is 11 minutes. The normal *minus 1* time is 6 1/2 minutes.

A rough analogy to this zone movement is equating the amount of light film receives to the amount of image that can be built. The more material (exposure) we have, the more image we can build. The lower the zone, the less raw material we have to build an image.

Developing the film until all of the material is used up in all of the zones is called total development. This is the maximum contrast that the film can produce but it is seldom used. Achieving the zone range that we refer to as normal almost never requires the maximum contrast that a film can produce. In virtually every case, the total development of a film would result in every f-stop difference being recorded as much more than a one zone difference. Films are manufactured with this potential in mind to allow greater developing flexibility. Figure 3.2 illustrates tone building and the development changes that influence it. The graphs are not intended to represent specific films, but are symbolic of general film responses. The build-up of the silver image is shown using a bar graph. The higher the bar of the graph the higher the zone.

MW 8

Exposing the film and developing it normally produces the normal zone relationship as in Figure 3.2 A. When the film is developed for a minus time, the high zones are not fully formed. They are moved down the zone scale and the negative will print with less than mormal contrast. A zone IX value might move down to a zone VIII and the print would show no pure white tone. The low zones show very little movement as seen in Figure 3.2 B.

When the film is given a plus development the high zones move upward dramatically while the lows show only a small movement, as in Figure 3.2 C. A zone VIII exposure value might move to a zone IX film value and print without tone. If the development is continually increased, the image material is eventually used up and the contrast can no longer increase.

The practical application of development changes is obvious when we observe their effects on a scene. Figure 3.3 B illustrates the scene as it appears when the film is developed normally. The lowest important value was placed on zone III and the selected high value measured four f-stops brighter and fell on zone VII. Figure 3.3 C shows the same scene as it appears when the film is developed to move the high value up one full zone, to zone VIII. The lower zones are basically unchanged, the middle zones have moved upward slightly, and the highest value has moved up the scale one full zone as planned. The contrast has increased.

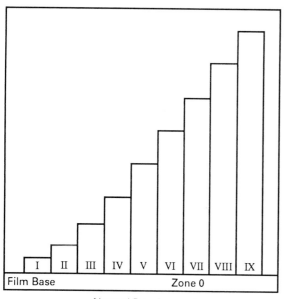

A   Normal Development

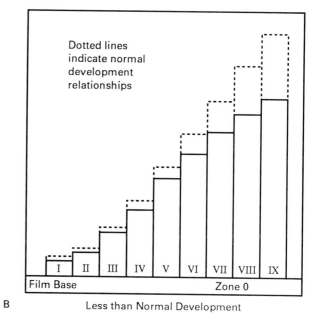

B   Less than Normal Development

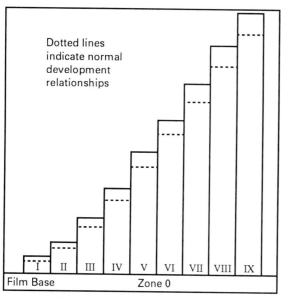

C   More than Normal Development

Figure 3.2 A,B,C *Bar graphs can be used to show the movement of zone relationships caused by development changes. Figure A graphs the relationship of tones with normal development. The higher the zone value, the higher the bar of the graph. Figure B shows the downward movement of the higher values when the development is less than normal. The lower zones are affected only slightly. Normal development relationships are indicated by dotted lines for comparison.*

In Figure C the high values move upward dramatically with greater than normal development while the lows move upward very slightly. Dotted lines indicate normal development relationships.

A   N-1 development

Figure 3.3 A,B,C *The effect of three different development times on negative contrast. In each figure the zone values are marked. Comparing Figure A (normal minus 1 development) to Figure B (normal development), we can see that the higher values are significantly darker when the development is decreased. In Figure C, a normal plus 1 development has moved the highest values upward to pure white in some cases. All prints were made on grade #2 paper and the print exposure was adjusted to match the zone III value so that high value movement could be compared easily.*

Figure 3.3 A is the scene as it would appear if the film was developed less than normal time. The lower values are very slightly weakened, the middle zones show some darkening in tone, and the high value has moved down the scale one full zone. These are examples of normal (N), normal plus one (N+1), and normal minus one (N−1) development. As indicated, the scene has been translated in three different ways. Movement of the high zones through development is complicated slightly because it takes different times to move different zones. The higher the zone the more it responds to development. Moving a zone VI to a zone VII might take 25%

MW 10

B   Normal development

Figure 3.3   *Continued.*

more development than normal, while moving a zone VII to a zone VIII might need only a 20% increase. Each film and developer combination has its own characteristics, and results from one film and developer combination may not apply to another combination. Deciding which zone to move is discussed in depth in Chapter 4 and the testing section.

By its nature, zone control is limited to accurately placing one lower value through exposure and developing to make one high value record as we want it. The two extremes are the only values that we control with good precision using exposure and development. We cannot, for example, use development to reverse zone relationships by making a dark object look lighter than a light object in the same scene. It is possible however, to accurately predict zone movements and relationships.

An old maxim of photography states, "Expose for the shadows and develop for the highlights." The Zone System verifies this general statement and gives us a way to restate with great clarity and accuracy: Place the low

C

N+1 development

Figure 3.3 *Continued.*

value using exposure because it cannot be moved much using development. Change the development when the high value does not fall where you want it in relation to the low value.

CHAPTER 3 SUMMARY

The ten step gray scale has a well textured (detailed) range of zone III to zone VII. Zones II and VIII also have tone but it is slight. This is the standard scale on which the Zone System is based. When we increase development we move the higher zones upward on the scale but the low zones are only affected to a slight degree. An increase in development beyond normal is called a *plus* development. If we move a chosen high zone up one full zone it is called a *plus 1* (N+1) development. A two zone move is called a *plus 2* (N+2).

Reducing development below normal is called *minus* development. Minus development moves the higher zones downward on the gray scale with little effect on the lower zones. When we move a chosen high zone down one full zone, it is called a *minus 1* (N−1) development. A two zone downward move is called a *minus 2* (N−2) development. Moving zones closer or farther from each other changes the contrast of the photograph. The higher the zone, the more it is affected by development changes.

Total development of the film means developing the film to its maximum possible contrast.

We can place one subject area on a low zone precisely and develop normally if the brighter subject area falls on the scale where we want it. If the brighter subject area falls on the scale where we *do not* want it, we can change the development from normal and move it to the zone value of our choice. Only one low zone and one high zone are precisely controlled.

TEST

Locate a sunlit, outdoor scene with large, single toned areas that can be easily measured and identified. A white painted house with areas in both sun and shade is excellent. Deep shadows under eves and dark shrubbery usually provide the needed low brightness areas. A measured difference of four to five f-stops between the important low and high brightnesses is ideal. Information on using the light meter accurately is found in Chapter 4. Determine the exposure by placing a large, easily measured area on *zone V* using the manufacturer's film speed. Try to find an object in about the center of the brightness range for placement. White paint in open shade is usually good. If sheet film is used, *make five identical exposures of the scene.*

Measure several other areas of the scene that are lighter and darker than the area placed on zone V. Note their difference in brightness. This can be done in terms of f-stops or EVs, but we must know where they should fall on the zone scale compared to the placed area. Measure as many parts of the scene as convenient, but be particularly careful to locate areas that correspond as closely as possible to zones II and III, and also zones VII and VIII. We will use these areas as reference points later but do not worry if nothing corresponds exactly to these zones, just note where they fall. A drawing of the scene may help you to mark zone relationships. The section on note taking offers an effective method of recording data.

Following your normal procedures, develop the negatives as indicated:

Negative #1—30% less than normal

Negative #2—15% less than normal

Negative #3—Normal (recommended by manufacturer)

Negative #4—15% more than normal

Negative #5—30% more than normal

On grade #2—paper print the *normally developed negative* so that the area placed on zone V matches the gray tone of a Kodak 18% gray card as closely as possible. Print all other negatives in an identical manner. Do not change print exposure or development. *Save these negatives and prints.*

If roll film or 35mm film is used, expose the entire roll at the same f-stop and shutter speed. Cut the film into five roughly equal strips and develop each strip as in the sheet film instructions.

Punching holes or cutting notches in the roll film strips aids in later identification. One notch or hole can indicate strip #1, two notches for strip #2, and so on. On sheet film, clipping off the corners of the film is easy, even in the dark. Clip one corner for sheet #1 and so on. For each development time, only one full frame of the roll film is needed for reference.

This test shows zone movement with development changes. It also provides information about the manufacturer's data about film speed and development. The zone relationships may not match the Zone System gray scale, but it is not necessarily wrong and only conforms to a different set of standards.

These negatives and prints should be visually evaluated and zone movements should be noted. Refer to the normally developed negative and write down approximately how much specific zones have changed with each development.

These negatives may be used for more accurate, sensitometric tests later.

Palm Leaves—Death Valley, California, 1983 *This scene required a normal plus 1 development. The two basic values in the scene were the palm leaves, placed on zone III, and the tiny white filaments growing from the ends of the leaves. The white strands were far too small to measure even with a spot meter so two negatives were made and marked for N+1 and N+2 development. After development the N+1 negative was selected for printing and the highs were rendered as zone VIII values.*

CHAPTER 4 Using the Zone System

Between theory and practice there are many subtle variations of procedure that can be used. Every step in using the system involves making decisions and applying technique correctly. The first three chapters offer an idealized Zone System that explains general principles but does not define the limits of actually using it.

The practicality of any system depends upon how much control is desired. The blend of intuition and technique is different for each photographer, and it is this difference, in part, that creates a personal photographic style. This blend will also change as your technical ability improves and your judgment is refined. Be as precise as possible in your use of the Zone System but don't expect absolute accuracy. You will probably enjoy more creative control than you have ever had, but this is a system of "zones", which implies some built-in tolerance. This section introduces some procedures of the Zone System, some of its limitations, and some of its problems.

PLACING ZONES

Placing a subject on a specific zone involves two major aspects: the emotional placement for creative purposes, and the technical procedure of getting the exposure right. Neither aspect can be neglected without serious problems occurring. The print may be technically perfect but may lack emotional significance, or we might know what we want and not be able to produce it. Usually we are looking for a combination of information and interpretation in photographs; the interplay of each is discussed here.

When we look at a scene, several factors influence the placement process. First, we scan the scene for the literal lightest and darkest areas. These may not be the actual areas that determine exposure and development but they must be considered as significant values. Even if they are regarded as accenting tones and not important enough to place, they can have a profound effect on the photograph. These areas may be too small and complex to measure with a light meter (see placement problems section), but the human eye is remarkably sensitive to extremely small changes in brightness and approximations can be made.

Next, it is crucial to locate the important low value of the scene. This is the subject area upon which we will base the exposure, the area we will *place*. We differentiate the literal low from the important low because they may not be the same part of the scene. (See Figure 4.1.)

The important low value does not necessarily mean a shadow or even a very dark area. It indicates a part of the scene that we consider important enough to insure precise placement. It is *usually* a shadow or dark area because these zones move so little with changes in development that the only effective control we have is placement. It is not uncommon to place an important low value as high as zone V if this is the value that must be recorded as a specific zone. Care must be taken when placing such a high

Important low value   Important high value

Literal low values   Literal high values

Figure 4.1   *The literal high and low values of a scene and the important high and low values are not always the same. The importance of a subject area must be determined by the photographer.*

The man's hair was selected as the important low value and placed on zone III. Basing the development on the white T-shirt was considered but it was decided that the light sections of the wall were more important to the scene. The light wall sections measured 4 f-stops higher than the hair and fell on zone VII. Normal development was selected.

The literal low values are the deep shadow areas of the engine. Although they could be placed on a detailed zone, it would force a minus development to retain detail in the light wall values which might weaken the overall effect of the scene.

The reflections in the engine chrome were the literal high values of the scene, but because of their size, detail or even a suggestion of tone were not needed. The literal extreme values of this scene were used as accenting tones.

Remember, these placements are personal choices. Though the brightness relationships of the scene are the same for anyone photographing it, the areas selected as important values may differ with the interpretation.

zone because it does move when the development is changed from normal. Other subject brightnesses can be measured and predicted, but only one brightness can be *placed.*

Most photographers work within the effective well-textured range of zone III to zone VII. This means they usually place the subject area they want to record as zone III and adjust the development to produce a zone VII tone for the important high textured value. Placing a zone 0 or a zone I is possible, but many materials have a very limited ability to distinguish between these extremely dark zones. With such small differences in tone even a minor mistake in measuring the light can destroy the separation between them. In effect, any tone below zone II becomes an accenting tone rather than an informational one. Placing a zone III value gives more flexibility in printing low values.

Once the important low value has been selected, it is measured and appropriate adjustments are made to properly place that value. If the exposure is made at this time, we would not know the relationship of the high value to the low, and development would be uncertain. The high value's position on the scale can sometimes affect how we place a low zone. The film may not be capable of the development that we plan and the placement might be altered.

If the film cannot record an extreme contrast range we might lower our placement to insure that the high values are recorded. This often happens when roll film is used and the entire roll must be developed to the same degree of contrast. Development adjustments are impossible for each scene and other compromises must be made. One alternative is to adjust the contrast grade of paper that is used. Using different contrast grades of printing paper is discussed in Chapter 5.

Now the scene is examined for the important high brightness. (Refer to Figure 4.1.) It may or may not be the lightest literal brightness of the scene. It is the area upon which we will base the development of the film. The brightness difference between the important low and the important high is measured and the zone scale position of the high value is noted. If it falls on the zone that we desire, the film is marked for normal development. If the high value falls on a zone that we do not want, the development is marked to move the value to the desired zone. Only one brightness in the scene can be precisely determined by development. Other areas record according to their brightness.

The process of placement and development determination takes more time to explain than to do. The entire sequence can be generalized into five short steps:

1. The scene is examined for the literal low value and the important low value. They are not always the same area.
2. The important low area is measured and placed on the desired zone by adjusting the exposure appropriately.
3. The important high value and the literal high value (if they are different) are located.
4. The difference between the important high value and the placed value brightness is measured and noted.
5. The final position of the high value is determined. The film is exposed and marked for development.

Remember, this is the *procedure* that is easily reduced to a few steps. The thinking process and camera operation are not so easily listed. Some of the difficulties of perception and technique are not so obvious.

Subject Placement Recommendations

It may be difficult to decide where to position subjects on the gray scale when the complexities of a real scene are encountered. As a visualization aid I have listed below the placements of general subject matter. I stress that these are only *recommendations* and that the imaginative rendering of scenes is a vital aspect of creative photography. Personal style is, in part, determined by your selection of appropriate zone positioning.

Zone 0   Pure black in the print. Primarily used as an accent tone, this value is not usually "placed." Small, deep cracks in wood or stone and objects silhouetted against a bright sky often fall on this zone.

Zone I   Very slight tone in print, often the effective pure black. This zone is usually regarded as similar to the zone 0 subject suggestions.

Zone II   Very deep shadows requiring minimal detail. Small areas of very dark foliage and doorway interiors that are not too prominent.

Zone III   Dark shadows needing full detail, deep rock shadows, dark black clothing or hair, or landscape shadows when a very graphic effect is desired. This is the most commonly placed value.

Zone IV   Skin values in shade, average foliage, dark stone, and large shadowed area in landscapes.

Zone V   Weathered wood, white paint in shade, clear north skies, and occasionally for dominant areas of open shade in landscapes.

Zone VI   Light stone in shadow, large, open areas of snow in shade. Some texts suggest this value for sunlit skin, but I personally find it too dark.

Zone VII   Light skin in sunlight, light rock values in sunlight, any area where full high value detail is required. This is the most common "target" zone for determining development.

Zone VIII   Brilliant snow, highlights on skin, white paint in sunlight (zone VII 1/2). This zone is occasionally a "target" for development though I don't recommend it for beginners.

Zone IX   Accent pure white. This value is seldom used as a target zone and use of it should be carefully considered. Scintillations on water or snow and glaring white surfaces are usually rendered as pure white.

Common Placement and Development Problems

Two problems occur regularly when students begin to plan their photographs. Both placement problems stem from the lack of experience in distinguishing the literal low value from the important low value. If the lowest possible brightness is placed to record detail when it should be used as an accent tone, the film is often overexposed dramatically. Many students use roll film and develop all of their film for normal contrast. Since they cannot vary development, they tend to ignore the high value as uncontrollable. The resulting negative is often unprintable because of the extreme overexposure. A subject area that should have been rendered as a zone 0 or I is placed on zone III or IV.

Conversely, the idea that all major shadows should be placed on zone III because zone III is the "right" tone for shadows can cause severe underexposure. The most common cases are large areas of open shade, the shadowed sides of buildings, and in portraiture, when a zone III placement of a facial shadow may be far too low for the average viewer. The important low may be an area that should be placed on a zone IV or a V value to be emotionally "correct."

These difficulties lie not in technical ability but in the understanding of how zone placement translates into visual terms. Many students are surprised at how dark a zone V tone actually appears in a print and a verbal description of zone III being "well-detailed" does not prepare them for the reality.

Another preoccupation of the beginner is "preserving detail" in the high and low values. On the surface it is a reasonable approach but it can endanger creativity. Pure white and pure black are not limited to roles as accenting tones. While they might not have detail they may be the correct zone for specific emotional effects. Even if they make up large areas of the photograph, subjects need not have detail unless the photographer wants it.

We list zone 0 and zone IX values as "zones" because they can be selected as a placed value or used as a development goal and are not necessarily to be avoided. It is appropriate to make any subject any tone you wish but *be careful*. Before you decide to record large areas as pure black or white consider the final effect and remember that if detail is not recorded on the negative it cannot be recorded on the print. If your personal requirements still dictate that you must move a zone VIII to a pure white zone IX, or place a subject on zone 0, then it is a valid visualization.

Sometimes a subject brightness will fall higher than zone IX. If the difference in brightness is large enough, a subject area can fall on any zone, though values above zone XI are rarely encountered. If a value is higher than zone IX, it just means that it will be pure white unless development is adjusted to record it as a zone below pure white (zone VIII or lower).

Where a subject falls is dependent upon your choice of what brightness is to be placed and on what zone. If a subject falls on zone XIII then the minimum development to record it as a detailed zone is a minus 5 development. This would reduce it to the highest detailed zone, print value VIII. This amount of reduction is impossible with normal processing methods. Refer to Chapter 5 for special processing procedures.

An extreme subject brightness can flare noticeably if it falls high enough on the scale. This appears as a "bleeding" of the high value into the adjacent lower tones.

Many times a beginner will treat an extreme brightness as an important high value. If brilliant highlights or direct reflections of sunlight are used to determine development the reduction may be too severe for the scene as a whole. Generally these brilliant highlights are used as accenting tones only. These areas are often the values that fall above zone IX. (See Figure 4.2.)

Another confusing area involves terminology. The designation "normal minus" development can apply to different zones and indicate different development times. Moving a zone VIII to a zone VII tone requires a different reduction in time than moving a zone VII to a zone VI. If we are communicating technical information we must be specific. This is especially important in classroom situations when one student is considering a movement of a specific zone and the instructor is talking about another zone entirely. Designating the zones by number avoids this problem.

It is also important to note that a designation of a three-zone *range* means a total of three zones, and a three-zone *difference* means that there is a total of four zones because we are measuring the space between zones. This is a problem with the distinction between the word "range" and the word

Figure 4.2 *When very small, even direct reflections of the sun will not measure as high a brightness as they will record. My spot meter suggested that these tiny points of light would fall on approximately zone VIII, but the meter was also measuring a considerable area of the dark water surrounding the reflection. A visual examination and personal experience told me that the reflections would exceed a zone IX value with my chosen placement.*

Except in carefully considered interpretations, specular reflections on water, glass, or metal should not be used as development references. The effect of flare must also be considered when scene values fall on extremely high zones.

I selected the dark grasses and the variations in the surface brightness of the water as my important scene values, and since their relationship was satisfactory for my interpretation the film was developed normally.

"difference" and this problem is not unique to the Zone System. It is also easy to infer that the chosen development indicates the actual subject contrast. This may not be the case since the film development is determined by personal choice. One photographer may interpret a scene as requiring normal development and a different photographer might indicate a normal plus 1 as the proper development for the same scene. Although the subject is the same, its contrast does not necessarily indicate what the development time should be.

Several zone devices have been designed to assist in visualization and exposure/development determination. These devices range in simplicity from a zone scale that is carried as a reminder, to fan-shaped "computers" that compensate for exposure corrections and development variations. Some photographers even use highly accurate gray scales of specific film and developer combinations. These aids can provide greater accuracy and control of the exposure/development process. If this approach appeals to you, some listings are available in the appendix under "Zone Calculators."

Mechanical Considerations

Zone prediction and recording involves operating the light meter correctly and transferring the data to the camera without error. People *will* make mistakes but they can be reduced in number by knowing where the pitfalls may be and using procedures that help minimize them.

Using EV numbers on light meters makes the calculation of brightness differences easy and rapid. The actual transfer to the meter dial can present some problems. Beginners often find it all too easy to move the dial the wrong way. An exposure that was intended to place a subject on zone III may accidentally result in an exposure placing it on zone VII. (See Figure 4.3.) Instead of a two f-stop *decrease* the film is given a two f-stop *increase*. Experience reduces the occurrence of errors.

Small plastic and paper zone scales have been designed for attachment to light meter dials. The EV number is set opposite the zone on which the subject is to be placed. Other subject brightnesses can be read directly on the dial. (See Figure 4.4.)

If the zone scales are not available or do not fit your type of meter (in-camera meters do not accommodate them) then the *zone V* placement reading can be transferred directly to the camera. All placement adjustments are then made with the camera controls. This avoids the intermediate step of using the meter dial and the potential of moving it in the wrong direction. It also reduces the chance of confusing the EV's with the f-stop numbers.

Many older cameras with through-the-lens metering read only in f-stop/shutter speed combinations. Often the only way to set exposure is to match two indicators by looking through the viewfinder and then at the camera controls. It can be hard to calculate brightness differences if both the f-stops and shutter speeds are changed to get readings. Unfortunately there is no solution except to be careful. Some equipment is not easily applied to the Zone System and it is important to investigate the practical use of any equipment you intend to purchase.

Newer cameras offer infinitely graduated shutter speeds but many have the traditional speeds which double or halve the exposure. If finer graduations are needed the f-stops must be used. On manually operated 35mm

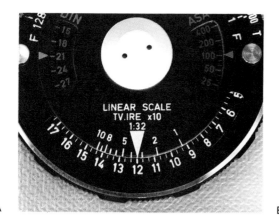

A

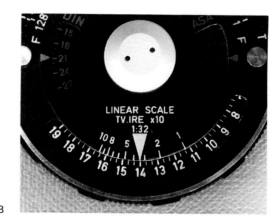

B

C

Figure 4.3 A,B,C   *Though using EV numbers simplifies the calculation of scene contrast, it does have some operational drawbacks.*

In Figure A the meter reading of EV 12 is located opposite the meter indexing mark. This would place a subject area measuring EV 12 on zone V. If we wish to place the value on zone III we must adjust the meter setting to find the f-stop, shutter speed combination.

Rotating the dial for a zone III placement would place EV number 14 opposite the indexing mark. This underexposes EV 12 by two f-stops, a zone III placement (Figure B).

Moving the dial the wrong direction causes a two f-stop overexposure, placing a subject measuring EV 12 on zone VII (Figure C).

Figure 4.4   *An example of a zone dial reminder on a common light meter. The measured EV can be set directly opposite the desired zone. This figure shows EV 10 placed on zone III and the location of other EV's in the scene can be read opposite the corresponding zone numbers. These reminders reduce accidental placement problems and are available from Zone VI Studios Inc., Newfane, Vt. 05345.*

cameras the f-stops are seldom graduated in less than 1/2 stop intervals and finer tuning is difficult using camera controls. Some electronic cameras have infinitely graduated f-stops and shutter speeds, though this precision is seldom encountered on the larger format cameras favored by most Zone System users. It is still necessary to check light meters in these graduated systems because though the meter may be precise, it can be just as easily precisely wrong as right.

Shutter speeds are often imperfect and should be checked before any testing begins. The simple mechanics of camera operation make precise negative consistency difficult if not impossible. When the variables of field work are added, the problems multiply. Filter factors, bellows extension factors, erratic shutters, and even weather conditions contribute to the photographer's difficulties. Even with the most precise testing, allowances must be made for negative inconsistencies due to mechanical realities.

Polarizing filters present their own special problems. All polarizers have some neutral density that reduces exposure, but the amount of neutral density differs from one brand of filter to another. The degree of polarization must also be considered. One area of a scene may be affected by only the neutral density because not all reflections can be polarized. Other objects are reduced in brightness by the neutral density *and* the actual polarization. Taking meter readings through the polarizer when it is set in the final picture-taking position is the only way to judge zone placement and contrast ranges accurately. If you wear polarized eyeglasses it can affect your assessment of subject brightnesses. Remove them for meter readings. This is particularly important when photographing large reflective surfaces or scenes that include water.

Because of design necessities the circular polarizers needed with the newer autofocus cameras tend to give slightly less polarization at maximum setting than standard polarizing filters.

NOTE TAKING

My priority in note taking is that it makes my system self correcting. I want enough information recorded to indicate why a problem occurred and to suggest a possible course of correction. If no technical information is available then problem solving is difficult and sometimes impossible. I recommend that some information always be recorded, especially during testing because it is assured that you will spend *less* time problem solving *with* notes than without them.

Typically the published information about photographs will read as follows:

Camera type—Nikon F-3

Lens used—50mm Nikkor 1:1.4

Film—Kodak Tri-X Pan @ EI 250

Exposure—1/125 sec @ f-16

Development—Kodak HC-110, dilution "B," 5.5 min. @ 68° F

For this information to be useful it must tell us something about how the photograph was made and how we can apply this data to our own methods to improve our photographic ability. At a minimum it should give us some clue as to what the photographer really wanted.

I am not suggesting that this particular information is useless, but it does not address Zone System priorities. It lacks a common reference point as a basis for comparison and it contains no data concerning the photographer's intent. Was this photograph planned or an accident? Where was the light measured and was that reading modified? How does the development relate to the contrast of the scene, etc.

The note-taking system in this chapter makes the photographer's creative intent its main priority and uses the Zone System's visual scale as a technical guide.

A sample exposure record is shown in Figure 4.5. It may seem complex but each bit of data is important. Cover each section carefully (there are only seven sections) because the price of poor note taking is that an error may go uncorrected.

Each section is explained here with suggestions on using the record for problem solving.

Scene A brief title or description of the photograph for identification. If sheet film is used, the film holder number may be identified here.

Film Type & EI This checks the meter setting and film speed. Use the actual working speed as determined by testing (the exposure index).

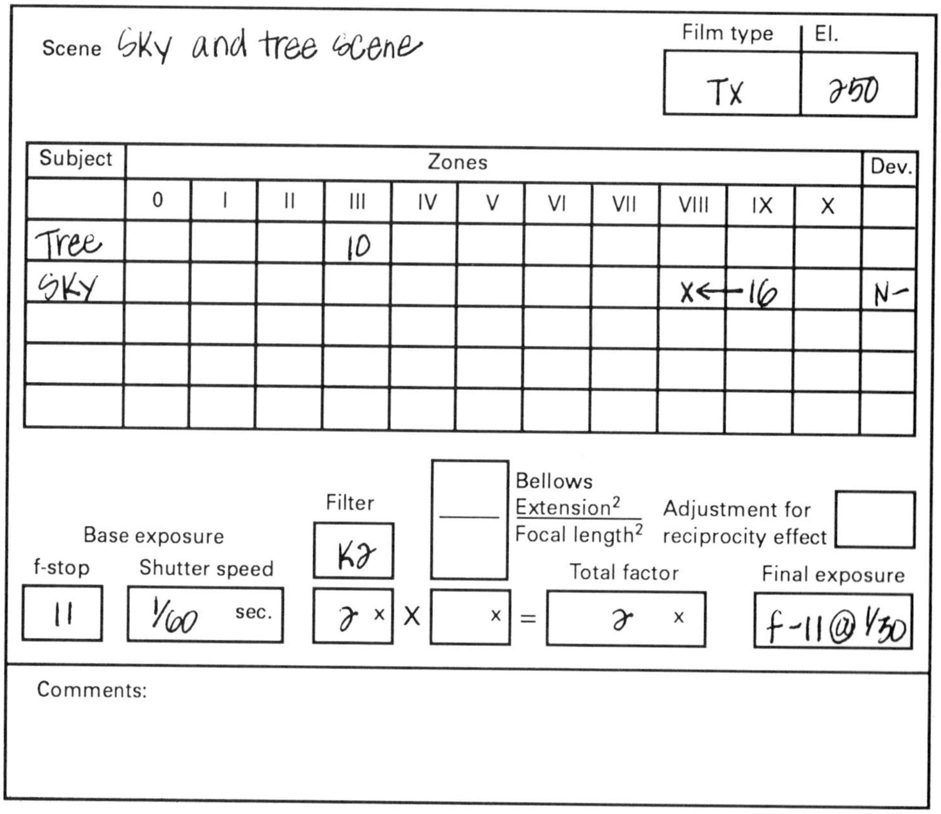

Scene Sky and tree scene

Film type: TX | EI.: 250

Subject	0	I	II	III	IV	V	VI	VII	VIII	IX	X	Dev.
Tree				10								
Sky									X←	16		N-

Base exposure: f-stop 11; Shutter speed 1/60 sec.

Filter K2: 2 × X [Bellows Extension²/Focal length²] × = Total factor 2 ×; Adjustment for reciprocity effect

Final exposure f-11 @ 1/30

Comments:

Figure 4.5 *Many versions of the exposure record may be designed for specific uses, but placements, development intentions, and their relation to subject area brightnesses should be included. Avoid shortcuts in note taking or the entire recording process may be invalid. A sample exposure record for copying may be found on page 144.*

Subject/Zone   This section shows the photographer's intent as well as recording data. It contains two vital pieces of information—the subject value that is placed and the value on which we have based the development. The subject is identified and the zone we place it on is marked. The sample is marked with the EV number that was read from the subject. This gives us a check on how well we transferred the meter reading to the camera controls. If your meter does not read in EV numbers then an "x" is used to mark placement. The placed value can be used as an exposure check as described later in this chapter.

Next, the important high value is marked on the zone where it falls with *normal* development. Use the EV number if possible. If the high value falls on the desired zone, no further notation is necessary here. If the high zone is to be moved by a development change, the planned development is indicated by drawing a small arrow to the desired zone. If a scene value falls higher than zone X, note its location and draw the arrow to the target zone.

In the sample, the sky falls on zone IX when the tree is placed on zone III. The notation shows that the photographer chose to move the sky value down to a zone VIII value. This indicates a normal minus 1 (N − 1) development. If it is desired, other subject areas can be measured and noted to check their movement. Only the placed value and the development value are vital.

Basic Exposure   The shutter speed/f-stop combination that is selected to place the low value.

Filter Factors and Bellows Extension Factors   Any filters used and their exposure factors are noted here. If a bellows extension compensation factor is needed it is also indicated. The bellows extension formula and filter information is included in the appendix. When more than one factor is involved they must be *multiplied*, not added like f-stops. The record serves as a reminder of this.

Filters affect both exposure and contrast and their use can significantly alter the planned development. The sample shows that a K-2 (yellow) filter was used with a factor of a 2X exposure increase. Since development was based on the sky's brightness, the contrast could be lower than meter readings indicate because of the filter's effect on the sky's color. No bellows extension factor is recorded on our sample so the total factor was 2X normal or one full f-stop more.

Adjustment for Reciprocity Effect   This can be expressed as an exposure factor or f-stop increase and affects both the exposure and contrast of the negative. The appendix has a detailed section on the reciprocity effect (also called reciprocity departure or failure).

Exposure Given   The actual exposure given to the film. This includes all filter, bellows extension, and reciprocity effect adjustments. The given exposure has little problem-solving value unless it can be cross referenced to the placed value, the brightness range, and the way the final print looks. With proper note taking an enormous amount of information can be related to the creative intent.

Using the Exposure Record

Let us suppose that the low value is accidentally recorded as a zone II value instead of the zone III that we planned in the sample exposure record. With a low value it is logical to suspect an exposure error. The low values are primarily controlled by the exposure, and even a relatively large development error will not seriously affect them. We can check this by an examination of the important high value of the negative. If the high value is wrong to the same degree and in the same direction, it is reasonably certain that the problem was one of exposure. You should recheck the film speed and the final exposure and cross-reference these to the meter EV to locate the problem. Even if you used the wrong film it can be checked. The only item that could not be checked is what exposure you actually set on the camera.

If the low value is recorded as planned but the high value is a full zone higher than you intend, there are two main suspects. The brightness difference may have been measured inaccurately or the development was too long. There are other possibilities but these are the most likely.

If a placed zone is *one zone lower* than planned and the important high zone is *one zone higher* than planned, a combination of underexposure and overdevelopment is probable. These deductions assume that the exposure record is correctly filled out.

These simplified examples demonstrate some applications of this data. The actual process of troubleshooting can be far more complex. If the possibilities for errors seem overwhelming, imagine trying to solve a problem *without* the notes.

With these notations the intended values are easily imagined. Questions and answers are related directly to the readers personal methods. Even if films, developers, and cameras are different from one photographer to another, it still gives visual references and an insight into the photographer's intentions. It is also a comprehensive record of how accurately the creative decisions were implemented.

Communicating Technique Through Notes

Because most Zone System workers use the same zone scale as a visual standard and use the same terminology, the communication of technical data is simplified. It is not only accurate in a visual sense, it is also applicable to changes in equipment, materials, and processes. It is like two people traveling to the same place but taking different routes. Both people will arrive at the same location though their journeys will differ.

Giving the f-stop, shutter speed, and development time is almost all the technical data we have come to expect as "complete." As far as applying this to our personal methods the information is virtually useless. Where was the meter reading made and how was it used? How does the development time relate to the brightness range of the scene? How can I use this information to learn?

The exposure record shows the photographer's intent, and through it the materials and processes can be cross-referenced. Two very different sets of materials can produce approximately the same results. Figure 4.6 lists the technical data for two different film/developer combinations that could produce the results in the sample record. Each places the same subject area

Record A

Scene Wall and Sky (test) "A"

Film type AGFA 25 | **EI.** 16

Subject	Zones											Dev.
	0	I	II	III	IV	V	VI	VII	VIII	IX	X	
Wall				12								
Sky								X ← 17				N-

Base exposure

f-stop	Shutter speed		Filter		Bellows Extension^2 Focal length^2	Adjustment for reciprocity effect		Total factor		Final exposure
32	1/4 sec.		x	X	x	=		x		f -32 @ 1/4

Comments: Develop in Rodinal 1+31
12 min @ 68° Agitation every 30 sec.
in small tank

Record B

Scene Wall and Sky (test) "B"

Film type TX | **EI.** 250

Subject	Zones											Dev.
	0	I	II	III	IV	V	VI	VII	VIII	IX	X	
Wall				12								
Sky								X ← 17				N-

Base exposure

f-stop	Shutter speed		Filter		Bellows Extension^2 Focal length^2	Adjustment for reciprocity effect		Total factor		Final exposure
32	1/60 sec.		x	X	x	=		x		f -32 @ 1/60

Comments: Develop in HC-110 1+31
4.75 min @ 68° Constant agitation in tray

Figure 4.6 *These exposure records show the same basic intention for placement and development. Aside from the inherent differences in the materials, each record indicates a combination of materials and processes that would produce approximately the same interpretation of the scene. The placement of subject values and the final print value relationship was intended to be the same.*

Without the exposure record's emphasis on the photographer's intent, it would be very difficult to compare technical successes or failures between the differing materials. Because the Zone System offers a consistent set of references, the intent can be compared to the result, and the accuracy of technical data can be cross-referenced.

on Zone III and records the important high value as Zone VIII. Both represent a normal minus development and both represent the intent of the photographer within the limits of the different materials.

There are, of course, aesthetic differences due to the inherent characteristics of the film/developer combination but the basic nature of the photograph would be the same.

This is not to say that accurate data can only be related in Zone System terms or that it should be used to duplicate photographs. It does demonstrate the usefulness of consistent reference points and the need for recording pertinent information. This exposure record is designed specifically for the Zone System, but it contains sufficient information for many other exposure and development systems.

Accurate data can be expressed in mathematical terms, illuminance ranges, or any number of ways. Each method can be precise but is based on a different priority for information.

USING THE LIGHT METER
The Spot Meter

Where and how light is measured significantly affects the accuracy of placement and the measurement of brightness difference. Contrary to merchandising claims, a spot meter does not automatically insure more accurate exposures. The measurement area is so small that a slight deviation in where the reading is made can cause large exposure errors.

In Figure 4.7 the curved oil tanks presented hidden difficulties. The light it not even from top to bottom or side to side. If we generalized these light and dark areas into a single zone, a one-degree spot meter could measure

Figure 4.7 *This type of situation can be deceptive when spot meters are used. The rounded tanks vary in brightness almost two zones, not including the direct sun reflection. Both the low and high value areas change in brightness from top to bottom and from side to side. There are even variations between individual panel sections of the tanks. Measuring the wrong area could result in a severe placement error or an incorrect contrast range assessment.*

The small glass insulators and even the telephone poles were too far away for accurate spot readings and could only be used as visual references for the other scene values.

Figure 4.8   *Open shade or overcast conditions do not guarantee low subject contrast or evenness of lighting. Brightness differences of almost two f-stops can be measured in different sections of the weathered wood. If the deep shadow of the window is used as the important low value, the specific section of the wall that is measured becomes important when determining subject contrast.*

If the camera position was moved to include background or sky it might be more logical to treat the general area of weathered wood as a single exposure zone by scanning the wall and averaging the readings.

the wrong part and an exposure error of a full f-stop could be made. Scanning the entire shadow and averaging the readings might be a more accurate exposure for these "zones" of brightness. If there is doubt about a specific area to measure, this scanning method may help. If this seems like a misuse of the spot metering concept it should be remembered that these meters are not designed to be more accurate than wide field meters. They only measure a smaller area and sometimes this is a drawback. Accuracy is dependent upon the use of the tool.

In Figure 4.8 the boards all have a slightly different brightness. If the lightest board is measured, the darkest board records almost two zones lower. Again, measuring the wrong board could cause an error in placement for the wall as a whole. Scanning the scene with the spot meter approximates the reading of a wider field meter.

The major difference between the spot meter and the wide field meter is usually one of convenience. The photographer need not approach the subject so closely when using the spot meter and readings can be made from the camera position.

The spot meter can also imitate the reading area of the wide field meter by scanning, or approximate the reading of an incident meter by measuring an 18% gray card. This versatility makes the spot meter the most common meter for Zone System use.

Figure 4.9 *A typical digital display in a 1-degree spot meter. The incremental dots indicate 1/3 f-stop changes in brightness. Some digital displays are difficult to read in bright sunlight. The newer, liquid crystal display models also show the readings in f-stops when desired. Increments as small as 1/10 f-stop can be read on some models. Gossen has recently introduced a meter that reads directly in zones.*

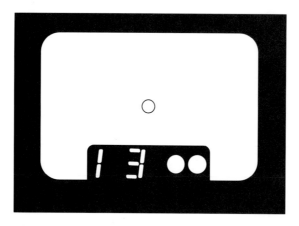

Figure 4.10 *Some meters read in a continuous scale using a needle to indicate EV numbers. Each line of this scale represents a 1/3 f-stop change in brightness.*

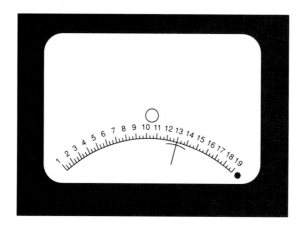

With digital technology comes the benefit of improved sensing cells and modern circuitry. Digitalization of the readings can have its own set of problems, however. In some digital displays it is difficult to see the 1/3 stop incremental lights when the meter is used in bright sunlight. (See Figure 4.9.)

While the 1/3 f-stop increments are sufficient in a majority of photographic situations, once in a while the difficulty of reading and the rather large incremental unit combine to make a significant exposure error. If you miss seeing an increment because of the difficulty in reading it in sunlight and the next increment is almost, but not quite lit, the exposure error may exceed 1/2 f-stop. This is not a theoretical problem, it actually occurs with some meters.

Older meters had internal, analog dials to display the EV numbers. (See Figure 4.10.) It was not only easy to read in most lighting situations but the f-stop graduations could easily be read in 1/4 stop increments or even smaller. They were, however, notoriously fragile and bulky.

The Wide Field Meter

I shall classify in-camera meters as a wide field meter even though the reading area changes with the lens used. Even the longest lenses in normal use do not approach the reading angle of a one-degree spot meter. Wide field meters usually measure an angle of approximately 20–45 degrees. For

Zone System use, the meter is usually moved close to the subject to fill the sensing area with a single subject. Often an object very close to the photographer is measured as a substitute if it matches a subject brightness in the scene. Special attachments, both factory and homemade, can be added to some wide field meters to convert them to a smaller reading area.

Wide field meters are often erroneously called averaging meters. In fact, they do not average values any more than any other meter but they do measure a larger scene area. The term averaging indicates the way they are commonly used—to measure the entire scene's brightnesses and give a Zone V exposure for that average.

The only general recommendation for light meter use and the Zone System is to read a single-toned subject area as carefully as possible. If this requires moving close to the subject or reading a substitute near the camera, I recommend it unless you are working in heavy mist or fog. In foggy conditions the intervening mist becomes part of the scene brightness and must be measured from camera position to avoid errors. Built-in camera meters work the same way as all other meters when the subject area that is measured is the same.

By comparing a planned (placement) exposure to an "averaged" exposure under various conditions, the difference between placing zones and mechanized exposures can be analyzed.

The Incident Light Meter and the Zone System

Incident light meters measure the light that illuminates or falls on the subject. They are also called illuminance meters or highlight meters. There is no way to directly measure actual subject brightness differences, so precise zone placement is difficult. For this reason they are not easily applied to the Zone System.

These meters employ a translucent dome or disc over the meter cell which transmits approximately 18% of the light to the cell. This reading is similar to measuring an 18% gray card under the same illumination with a reflected light meter. It is suggesting an exposure that will place an 18% gray card on a zone V. Other subject brightnesses fall in relation to this medium gray object. Because we do not know precisely where the other subject areas will fall on the scale the only direct application to the Zone System would involve knowing the actual reflectance of the subjects. We could then determine how much lighter or darker than a gray card each object is, and their gray tones could then be predicted.

The incident meter is designed to favor the high values of a scene. That is, it suggests an exposure that will make a gray card zone V and it is designed for making readings in an even illumination level like direct sunlight. The 18% gray card is actually somewhat lighter than the average subject brightness in even light. If it renders the gray card as Zone V in bright sun, it insures that even very reflective subjects in sunlight will be recorded with detail. In the same scene, a very dark object like black velvet *in shade* would fall far below Zone I. It would not be recorded as a textured tone. As you can imagine, using an incident meter for Zone System placement is tricky.

Several ingenious methods have been developed to use the incident meter to measure subject brightnesses with varying degrees of success. Most of these methods, like all systems, have advantages in certain situations and their own built-in problems.

The incident meter is most useful for measuring illumination levels at a specific subject area. It is not limited to this function but is designed for it. Its use in creative photography should not be underestimated and any serious student of photography should investigate the applications of the meter. It is not however, the most appropriate instrument to use with the Zone System.

General Light Meter Cautions

Light meters, like all machinery, have their failings. Some will give a zone V exposure in most situations but deviate when the light level is very low or very high. A meter that always reads the same zone is considered "linear" in operation. The cost of a light meter is no guarantee of linearity. Any meter can be tested by a technician or through practical comparisons of negative densities. Negative densities from very low and very high light levels can be compared to densities from subjects of average illumination levels. If a substantial difference exists in these extreme cases it is reasonable to suspect non-linearity. Several tests may be necessary to eliminate the possibilities of erratic shutters, the effect of reciprocity failure, flare, and human error.

A meter can also be compared to a known meter if its linearity can be trusted. Most high quality meters are built to sufficient tolerances for practical work. *Meter accuracy is essential for testing.*

With some older meters irregular color response is possible as is the temporary blinding of the meter by pointing it at an intense light source like the sun. Newer instruments are less prone to these problems.

Shield the meter from direct sun when making measurements. Spot meters and in-camera meters both have glass as part of their systems and are subject to flare. Some in-camera meters are also very sensitive to stray light entering through the eyepiece and care is necessary to avoid inaccurate readings.

The procedure for determining what zone your meter reads is described in the testing section. This calibration is essential before any accurate tests can be made. Meter variation from a zone V reading can be substantial.

CHAPTER 4 SUMMARY

When placing zones, the distinction between the important low and the literal low zone must be considered. They are not always the same.

Development determination is also based on selecting the appropriate subject area. The literal high value of a scene may not be the important high value. Basing the development on brilliant scintillations or reflections may cause underdevelopment for the scene as a whole.

The selection of the subject areas considered important determines, to a large extent, the aesthetic qualities of the photograph. Different interpretations of a scene may result in different subject areas being used as references for exposure and development.

The Zone System note-taking method addresses the relationship of the photographer's creative intent, the subject's physical characteristics (brightness range etc.), and the camera settings needed to produce the desired effects (the technique).

The note-taking method allows accurate communication of technique between photographers because it relates a visual goal to personal techniques and materials. When the technical standards and terms are consistent, communication of technical information is improved. Problem solving is much easier when the technical information can be cross-referenced to a specific visual goal.

The subject area that is measured by the light meter significantly affects the accuracy of the planned exposure. Great care is needed in determining the appropriate subject area to measure with spot meters; they measure such a small area that errors can occur with complex subjects. Spot meters are not more accurate than wide field meters, but they are usually more convenient for Zone System use because they can measure small areas from the camera position.

The incident light meter is designed to measure illumination levels and is difficult to apply to Zone System use. It is *not* inferior to reflected-type light meters but is designed for different photographic applications.

TEST

Compare several exposures for your personal placement of subject values to exposures of the same scene made by other (non-Zone System) methods to see how they differ. Make the non-Zone System determination first so it does not affect your placement choices.

Examine the Zone System notes of another photographer before viewing the photograph. Try to visualize the relationship of general tone values from the notes. Cross-reference the data to your own materials and methods if they differ, and determine the method you would need to produce the same tone relationships.

Mud and Reflections— Perris, California, 1981 *This photograph posed a number of difficulties that are commonly encountered in field photography.*

1. Because the mud was very close to the camera, a bellows extension factor was needed to insure correct exposure.

2. The background reflection is of a corrugated building about 20 feet away. A small f-stop was needed to maintain enough depth of field for a relatively sharp recording of the reflection.

3. The small f-stop required an exposure time of one second, but the water was occasionally moved by gusting wind and I had to make the exposures between gusts. The wind also made meter readings of the high values difficult because it "broke up" the reflection which gave false readings.

4. The exposure time required a small adjustment for reciprocity failure.

5. The mud was in deep shadow while the building (reflection) was in bright sun, requiring an N — 1 development.

CHAPTER 5   Materials and Processes

PHOTOGRAPHIC PAPERS AND CONTRAST CONTROL

So far the film's response to exposure and development has been discussed without regard to the paper it will be printed upon. As with the definition of normal development there are variations in the definition of a normal paper. The total number of zones and the actual relationship of the zones that can be printed is dependent upon the brand, contrast grade, paper developer and our personal handling of the photographic process. We can expose and develop a negative to precise technical standards, but it may not reflect our visualized intent unless it is customized to the known characteristics of a printing paper.

The Zone System definition of normal development is based on being able to print a certain number of zones on a specific grade of paper. It is possible to tailor a negative to print on almost any contrast grade of paper with reasonable accuracy. The exposure/development process is flexible enough to accommodate great differences in paper contrast, but by tailoring the negative to a single grade we can use the paper grades to raise and lower contrast when other methods fail or are unavailable. The contrast differences in paper were designed as an alternative to altering contrast by development and offer a major method of creative control in printing.

MW 16

At the end of each chapter and in the testing section, one of the criteria is that the negatives are printed on a contrast grade #2 paper. This is the accepted normal grade by industry standards. Like the concept of medium gray being a value of 18% reflectance, the basis for this decision is complex but the reasoning for these choices need not be understood for practical use.

The grading of papers is somewhat arbitrary. The only consistency between brands that carry the same grading is that the higher the grade number the higher the contrast. The number of paper grades available differs with the brand of paper but generally runs in numbers from 0 to 5. The only reliable reference point is that a higher number refers to a higher contrast. A grade #3 paper always has more contrast than a grade #2 paper of the same brand.

Standardizing on a grade #2 paper puts paper grading into the perspective of Zone System terminology. We tend to think of the print as the final product of the photographic process but changing paper grades is also a contrast control like changing development. Examined in the context of a contrast controlling method, we can discuss the paper's effect as we would discuss development changes.

Using Paper Grades
Approximates
Development Changes

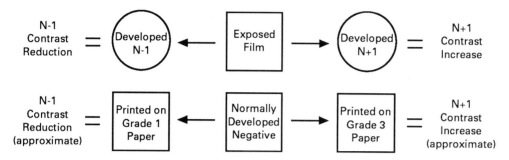

Figure 5.1 *Changing contrast grades of paper affects the contrast of the image in approximately the same manner as development changes. This figure is idealized in the sense that a change in paper grade does not always equal a full plus or minus development.*

Development Changes
Combined With Paper Grades
To Extend Contrast Control

Figure 5.2 *Paper grades and development changes can be combined to make contrast changes beyond the level that can be achieved by either method alone. Again, the diagram indicates a paper grade equalling a full plus or minus development, but this may not occur with some brands of paper.*

If a normal zone relationship is obtained by printing on a grade #2 paper, it follows that printing the same negative on a grade #3 paper would increase the contrast of the final print. This approximates the effect of plus development by moving the zones farther apart. The precise amount of movement is determined by the paper's characteristics and its processing. If the same negative is printed on a grade #4 paper the contrast increase is greater. Figure 5.1 illustrates the paper's effect by comparing it to development changes.

In the illustration each paper grade has been idealized as equalling a one zone movement. This may not be the actual amount of movement in practice.

Figure 5.1 also demonstrates the reduction of contrast through paper grades and the approximate equivalents to decreased development.

When different paper grades are combined with the development of the negative, the effect on contrast is cumulative. Contrast compactions and expansions are extended beyond what either method could accomplish alone. Figure 5.2 illustrates this cumulative effect.

This flexibility allows photographers using roll film and 35mm cameras to use Zone System terminology. Even if the film development cannot be adjusted to each individual scene, the visualization process still applies. Communicating technical information is also easier when the Zone System references are used.

If we specified *grade #3* paper as our *normal* grade, exposure and development of the film would have to be different to produce the normal scale. Grade #3 paper cannot reproduce all of the zones in a negative scaled for a grade #2 paper because the negative has too much contrast. Decreasing the development of the negative and lowering its contrast can approximate the normal zone scale on the grade #3 paper. Many photographers using 35mm films scale negatives to print on a grade #3 paper because less film development, which produces finer grain, is needed. What is lost is some of the ability to expand the print contrast by using paper grades. Some paper brands do not exceed a grade #4 contrast and standardizing on a grade #3 limits contrast increases to only one grade higher.

Some modern films cannot increase contrast more than a plus 1 expansion. If the negative is scaled to a grade #2 paper we can expand it two graduations higher using higher paper grades.

By tailoring the negative to a specific brand and grade of paper we can change contrast in both directions and favor the direction where the films do not perform well.

Variable contrast papers work like graded papers with the distinct advantage of more subtle graduations of contrast. The special filters used to vary contrast are available in ½ grade increments, and by using color printing filters or dichroic color enlarging lights the graduations become even more subtle. Local dodging and burning may be done using different filters to provide even greater control.

MW 13

The fine points of printing are too numerous to include in a Zone System text. A more general concept is more important and is directly related to the system; any contrast change can be related in Zone System terms no matter what causes them. A major function of the Zone System is to provide a fluid method of communicating photographic technique that does not involve more than a practical knowledge of sensitometry. I must emphasize that the greater the understanding of sensitometry the greater the possibility of creative control. The Zone System places an emphasis on interpretation as the goal of technique and it is ultimately a practical application of sensitometry and not the science itself. It is important to note that it was a complete understanding of the sensitometric process that allowed the Zone System to be conceived in the first place.

Visual Assessment of Print Contrast

Assessing the effect of paper grades visually is tricky. The number of zones that fit on a grade #2 paper won't record on a grade #3 if all other factors remain constant.

Using development we can increase the contrast of the paper only to a minimal degree. The general effect of overdevelopment is to darken all tones in approximately the same manner as increasing the exposure. Underdevelopment of the print will decrease the contrast but it usually does not allow the paper to produce the maximum black that it normally produces. The most practical approach is to change the grade of paper to accommodate our visual needs or to use an entirely different paper/developer combination. Low contrast developers are readily available but paper grading allows the use of a single developer for a variety of negative interpretations.

Often the lower zones are merged by extending the development times. The zone II and zone I values are darkened by the development, and the larger dark area gives an illusion of greater contrast due to its sheer size. The low zone values may merge into a large area of zone 0 tone.

MW 14   Attempting to print a negative scaled for a grade #2 paper on a grade #3 can be deceptive in a slightly different way. If a paper will only record 4 zones and we try to print a negative that has a 5 zone textured range (normal), one zone cannot be recorded on the paper. Adjusting the printing exposure to maintain detail in the *high zone* will force the lower zone beyond the paper's ability to record it. If the exposure is adjusted to preserve the *low zone* detail, the high zone does not record. In visually judging the prints the conclusion about which zones were affected might run either way. In the print that was adjusted for the high zones it might be thought that only the low zones were affected because they are now too dark. In the second case the low zones have been adjusted to maintain proper detail and the high zones are wrong. This demonstrates that while visual evaluation of prints is valid in an emotional sense, it can be very misleading when looking for technical accuracy. The paper grade affects the entire scale, not just the high zones or the low zones. Visual assessment of negatives and prints and its problems are discussed in the testing section.

The contrast of papers not only differs from brand to brand but so do less tangible factors that influence the appearance of the print. The print color, the maximum black, the surface texture and the whiteness of the paper stock change with the type and grade of paper even within the same brand. The advent of "fine art" papers in recent years has further complicated the selection process because they have slightly different characteristics than the more common "commercial" papers. The variations can complicate testing and I strongly recommend that students standardize on a single paper type as well as one film type. These examples also support the notion that "normal" is a relative term even when applied to specific brands of materials.

Selection of Films for the Zone System

Aside from the usual considerations of film speed, sharpness, and grain size, selecting a film for Zone System use involves its ability to expand and contract zone relationships as development is changed. Since we attempt to control negative contrast instead of relying on paper grades, the amount of potential plus and minus development is important. We must also consider the total amount of movement and the practical factors of working time, availability and actual handling of the materials. The development time for a plus two contrast increase may be so long that the working time becomes inconvenient or a film's reciprocity characteristics may not suit our needs. Some films may present difficulty in handling because of a thin

MW 8   base material or may not be available without making special bulk orders.

There are no easy answers but almost any popular film moves one full zone up or down with only minimal exposure correction, and development times for this movement are seldom extreme.

MW 18   The tabular grained films are unusually responsive to development changes and the potential for contrast control is considerable when compatible developers are used.

Extreme movements of plus or minus two or more may require special films or procedures which are described later in this chapter.

The final consideration of film selection is intangible because it deals with a visual evaluation of the photograph. It is possible to achieve the proper technical relationships of the zones and then have the print look "wrong." Usually this is a visualization problem or a simple dissatisfaction with the print in general, but occasionally it is inherent in the film and developer combination that you use. The final judgment of creative work is an emotional one and film/developer combinations do have differences that measuring devices cannot assess. Most of these distinctions are subtle and even experienced photographers have difficulty in deciding when it is an inherent film/developer characteristic problem, a procedural error or a visualization difficulty. Blaming the materials is usually the best way to insure that the problem does *not* get solved. A patient reevaluation of personal technique often resolves any quality problem of such a subjective nature.

These assessments can range from the low values appearing weak or "muddy"-looking to an inability to see subtle changes in the high values. These areas of the gray scale are the extremes and do not record with the same distinctions as the middle values. These extremes are the parts of the gray scale that differ the most from film to film. A zone II density on two different films may look slightly different when printed because of the relationship of the other extremely low values within the zone. High zones may appear chalky or lacking in detail due to film characteristics or incorrect development time. It is very difficult to know the reason without experience *and* testing.

Printing paper characteristics must also be considered because it is not always possible to judge how a film density will look in subjective terms.

Information concerning the movement potential of films and the exposure compensation needed can be determined by an examination of the characteristic curves of the film. These curves are diagrams of a film's response to exposure and development. They can save enormous amounts of time and energy if used instead of trial and error testing. Characteristic curves are discussed in the sensitometry section of Chapter 8.

If you cannot read curves, then personal testing or the advice of other photographers must be used to assess development possibilities.

The general suggestions that I can make for selecting a film are:

1. Select a readily available film and developer combination from a single, major manufacturer. Developers and films from different manufacturers will mix but are not necessarily designed for each other. Your assessment of film contrast potential will probably be based on information that *does not* include cross-over film/chemical combinations.
2. Avoid exotic developers, films or processes. There are no magical formulas or combinations and most traditional combinations will give at least a movement of one zone up or down in contrast.
3. Assess the film from a standpoint of potential contrast control as well as grain size, sharpness and speed.

MATERIALS AND PROCESSES
FOR CONTRAST CONTROL

In selecting photographic materials and the processes that manipulate them, our criteria should be as specific as possible. It is not only practical that we know the limits of the system under normal conditions but also the alternatives when our creative choices exceed what normal methods can produce.

If exposure compensations are made, the contrast of film can be changed by simple increases or decreases of development time. Frequently the exposure adjustments are less than ½ stop to maintain a zone III value for a one zone movement up or down.

As the changes become larger, as in a minus 2 or plus 3 development, so does the need to modify normal methods or change the materials that become less and less effective. The standard processes for controlling contrast are described in the testing section. This chapter discusses options that extend our technical controls beyond normal limits and emphasizes techniques and materials that are relatively common and easy to use.

Reducing Contrast

Contrast changes beyond one zone may require special handling of both the film and the processing. The extreme reduction of contrast is possible by using procedures that develop values disproportionately. These techniques provide a relatively normal development to the low zones while restricting the development of the high zones. The result is a reduction of overall negative contrast with a minimum loss of low zone quality. Exposure compensations are also kept to a minimum because the development of low zones is more efficient.

MW-P 20

Although superceded by the use of highly diluted developers and special agitation patterns, the water-bath process illustrates the use of applied technique in creative photography and is the basis for more current approaches to controlling high contrast situations. It involves the repeated transfer of the film from the developer to plain water and back again. The film is first saturated with developer and placed in water without agitation. The heavily exposed areas (high zones) exhaust the developer more rapidly than the slightly exposed low zones. Relatively normal development is attained in the low zones and the highs are reduced to a great degree. Because the water-bath process requires the film to lie flat in the solutions, it is impractical for roll film use.

MW-P 19

For roll and 35mm films it is more practical to utilize a variation of this thinking called the two-solution process. The film is transferred from the developer (usually only once) to a mildly alkaline solution and agitated only minimally or not at all. The alkalinity of the second bath favors continued development, but the high zones react as in the water-bath and stop developing while the lows continue to build. The contrast decrease is very controllable and the alkalinity of the second solution insures enough developer activity that the film need not lie flat. Roll film can be processed in conventional tanks.

The most practical and simple method for sheet film contrast reduction uses a very dilute developer and modified agitation patterns. For a large portion of the development time the film is not agitated. This "still time" promotes the same effect as the water-bath process. The developer cannot be replenished without agitation and it acts as if the film was placed in a water-bath. It is a bit tricky to determine the proper dilution/agitation combination and if the agitation interval is too long the development may be uneven. Still times exceeding 1 ½ minutes should be avoided. Highly diluted developer may cause streaking unless the film remains flat and motionless during the still time. Tray processing is recommended.

MW 11

MW-P 21

Kodak T-Max and the Ilford Delta films are extremely sensitive to agitation changes and prolonged still times may cause uneven development. I do not recommend agitation intervals beyond a *maximum* of one minute when using these films.

It is important to note that the more extreme the dilution of a developer the more quickly disproportionate development occurs. The developer that is absorbed is used up more rapidly because it is weaker, so the agitation interval that produces disproportionate development changes with dilution.

With most extreme contrast reductions some exposure increase is needed since no process is 100% efficient. The disproportionate development techniques will reduce the amount of exposure increase needed to maintain low value detail over conventional methods.

Increasing Contrast

Most modern films will expand to a plus one contrast with conventional development increases, but some will not move to a plus two without modifications of technique or special developers. As the development is extended there is also an increase in grain size and the danger of fogging due to prolonged development.

When the film will not increase in contrast enough for our needs or if grain size becomes a problem, a high contrast film may be substituted for the standard materials. Personally, I find it easier to use a different film and a standard developer instead of using a high energy developer which can be erratic and does not solve the problems of grain size or potential fogging.

Kodak Technical Pan film or graphic arts films (sometimes called lithographic films) can yield finer grain, sharper images, and a much greater potential for contrast increases than conventional films.

Since these films are designed to produce extreme contrast, most of the practical technique involves developing the films for less than their "normal" times. "Normal" for these films produces images of ultra high contrast. In order to make negatives of plus two, plus three, or even plus four contrast ranges, it is necessary to develop the film to less than its total potential and actually use processing methods usually reserved for *reducing* contrast.

A common field application may involve a scene with a brightness difference of only three f-stops from the literal low to the literal high value. With conventional films, placing the low value on zone II would mean that the highest subject value falls on zone V. Not only is a zone V value too low to be moved easily by development, it ignores the fact that there are no subject areas that record as zones 0 or I. (See Figure 5.3.)

A

B

Figure 5.3 A,B   This is the same scene recorded on a normal and a high contrast film. Figure A was made on Tri-X sheet film and developed normally. Figure B was made on Technical Pan sheet film and developed to an N+3 contrast. Even if Tri-X film could expand to this degree of contrast, the grain would be visible in all but the smallest print sizes.

These prints were made to maintain a pure black in the deep rock cracks so that a comparison of a maximum number of print values could be made.

Interpreting this scene with a full scale of zone values requires a greater contrast increase than most films can produce even using the highest paper grade and development combinations. Other contrast increasing possibilities are discussed in the appendix.

With conventional films a contrast increase of this magnitude means that the low value placement must be very precise. It must be low enough that it won't respond to the development but not so low that it loses detail. Accurate meter readings are essential, and even with perfect placement the increase in grain size may be a problem even with large format negatives.

Because they are fine grained by nature, the high contrast films reduce grain problems and the need for using extremely high paper grades. Possibly the greatest difference in visualization with these films is their unusual response to colors. Technical Pan film has an extended red sensitivity. It records red as very light or white. Graphic arts films are mainly sensitive to blue and green light and do not "see" red at all. Technical Pan film can be made to approximate a panchromatic response by adding cyan filtration (about 40 cyan) during exposure but it is tricky in the field to judge how much filtration is correct. Graphic arts films are very slow (about ISO 6) and their color response so extreme that I do not recommend attempting any corrective filtration.

MW-P 22

Both films are available on thin base material which can make the loading of roll film on reels and tray development of sheets a little difficult. To prevent slippage of the sheet film in the film holders, the holder can be tapped gently to reposition any suspicious film.

Due to its static electricity properties, the base material of this film also seems to be more prone to dust spots than other films. Extra care is needed to protect it from dusty field conditions.

CHAPTER 5 SUMMARY

The Zone System definition of a normally developed negative is based on the number of zone values that will record on a contrast grade #2 printing paper. We adjust the development of the negative to accommodate the characteristics of the printing papers we are using. These adjustments also promote a consistency of negative quality in both visual and technical terms.

By standardizing on a grade #2 paper we can increase or decrease the contrast of the photograph by using other paper grades. It is possible to standardize on another grade of paper but some contrast control potential is lost because papers come in a limited number of grades. Using a grade #2 paper usually allows sufficient contrast control both upward and downward.

Paper grading is used as an alternative to adjusting negative contrast by development or to supplement development control. Development changes and paper grading can be combined to extend our control of the contrast of the photograph.

Any contrast changes can be thought of and discussed in Zone System terms. Lower than normal contrast grades (0–1) approximate the effects of minus developments while higher than normal paper grades (3–5) approximate the effects of plus developments.

Variable contrast papers use filters to vary the contrast of the print. They can change contrast in smaller increments than graded paper, and it is possible to vary the contrast of localized print areas by using more than one filter grade on the same print.

A special consideration in selecting a film for Zone System use is the amount of contrast change that can be accomplished by development changes. Most films will move at least to a plus 1 or a minus 1 contrast change with simple development time changes. Extreme situations may require unusual processing procedures or the substitution of a specific film type.

The concept of disproportionate development is illustrated in the water-bath process and a more current method based on this approach uses highly diluted developers and modified agitation techniques. Two solution development is a form of disproportionate development. Disproportionate development techniques are usually used for extreme contrast reductions or for greater efficiency in normal methods.

Special high contrast developers may be used for extreme contrast increases, or special films such as Kodak Technical Pan or graphic arts films may be substituted. These films have the advantage of ultra fine grain and sharpness but also have unusual color responses that must be considered.

TEST

Test A Photograph a scene of low brightness difference on a high contrast film and a conventional film with a potential of at least a plus 2 contrast increase. Develop both films to the same contrast (at least normal plus 2) and compare grain size and image sharpness.

Test B Using the film type, make two identical exposures of a scene with a high brightness difference and develop each film for a normal minus 2 contrast decrease. Make *no exposure correction* for low zone movement. On one negative use a reduction of development time *only* with no special agitation procedures, and on the second negative use one of the methods of disproportionate development. Compare the density of the low zones to determine the effectiveness of disproportionate development.

If you do not know the correct development times for your film consult the testing section for procedures. MW 10 has information about exposure compensations for extreme contrast reductions.

CHAPTER 6 Myths and Standards

T he Zone System has been variously described as "too technical," "not technical enough," "too mystical," and "too pragmatic." None of these observations applies to the craft involved in the Zone System. They refer to personal ideas about how technique can be applied to making photographs. The system was designed to facilitate creative control and not limit it to a dogma of politics. The misconceptions about the system are many and some are discussed here.

Without an understanding of the Zone System ideas and methods it is difficult to understand *why* some of these statements are myths. If the reasons are unclear refer to Chapters 1–4 for further information.

MYTHS ABOUT THE ZONE SYSTEM

The Zone System is Too Slow and Complicated Many beginners have the impression that many meter readings and complex calculations are needed to use the Zone System. Actually only two meter readings are needed to determine exposure and development. The only difference in metering technique is that the photographer must make a decision as to where to place the subject on the zone scale. This choice is what makes a photograph personally expressive. The time spent checking other values in the scene is a matter of experience and precision.

Photographers can choose the limits of applied technique for themselves. I have found that it may require a few extra seconds to make these choices but it rarely consumes any significant time. Experienced photographers can estimate brightness ranges without light meters and the most that might be required is to make one more reading of the high value to determine development. All that is left is to write down the development that is wanted. It is always possible to blindly follow the meter but even people who don't use the Zone System often modify the exposure based on their experience.

The Zone System Only Works with Large Format Cameras As far as the Zone System is concerned the only difference between large and small cameras is when one sheet of film can be developed at a time. Single sheets can be developed precisely for each scene. Roll film requires a more general approach. Roll film restrictions can be overcome with extra camera

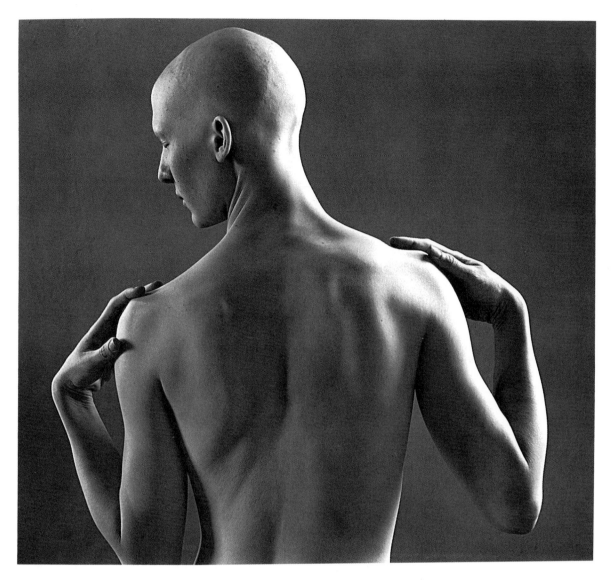

Frances—1979 *Because of other frames on the roll, this 120 film was scheduled for an N — 1 development. Adjusting the contrast was done by moving the model between the light sources (two windows, one on each side of the model).*
The shadowed areas of her back were placed on zone V and for this photograph she was moved to obtain a zone IX value on the highlighted skin. The N — development reduced the skin values to zone VIII.
This illustrates that even when the procedure does not involve development controls (the entire roll was developed to N — 1 regardless of scene contrast), Zone System thinking and terminology can still be applied to photographic situations.

bodies, interchangeable backs, different paper grades, special developing methods, etc. Even if an entire roll must be developed to the same contrast it does not negate the idea of contrast control. We must use methods other than development changes to accomplish it.

Zone System Methods Force a Preoccupation with Technique   It is the photographer who decides how much technique to apply. If an exposure and development system dictates how much technique is needed, then control of the photograph is no longer in the hands of the photographer. Any method of this nature should be discarded by anyone wanting creative control. Most Zone System workers don't think of their technique in terms of "how to" because they know how the materials react. For them the difficulty lies in making creative choices. It is difficult to hide behind excuses if a photograph does not appear as predicted. I think most encounters with the Zone System involve very technical approaches to the craft. This is not necessary but it does further the myth that only a mathematical genius can understand and use the Zone System. It is unfortunate that it is assumed that one approach to craft is the only approach. The entire philosophy of the Zone System is geared to allow the photographer to set personal, technical limits.

The Zone System Makes All Your Photographs Look the Same as Other Zone System Worker's   This thinking assumes every photographer will make the same aesthetic decisions. It also assumes it is possible to precisely communicate technique so it can be duplicated. While the second assumption may be true in a tonal sense, it disregards composition and equipment, not to mention the amazing diversity of personal tastes. This criticism may be directed more at the most common use of the system— *photography in the field.* These are methods that control the materials (films and developers) rather than the light and are most useful when the light is not within our control, as in field photography. It would be equally unrealistic to say, "If you don't use the Zone System you can't photograph in the field."

The Zone System Is Only Good for Scenic Photography   Understanding exposure and development applies to all kinds of photography— outdoor or studio, artistic or technical. We can place a skin tone in a portrait or develop for more contrast in a scientific photograph. The terms are designed for artistic communication but the responses of the film remain the same. This is a method of controlling materials, and the kind of photograph we choose to make is irrelevant.

The Zone System Requires a Light Meter   This section requires a strong disclaimer. For the great majority of photographers this statement is *true* in a practical sense. Determining exposure and development can be by light meter or estimation but before you throw away your light meter you should make sure you have the skill to do without it. I have learned to think in terms of zones and I know many photographers who can estimate exposures with remarkable accuracy and consistency. The Zone System is as much a way of *thinking* about photographic technique as it is a method of controlling it.

Light meters are not necessarily more accurate than an educated guess. They can be used improperly or malfunction; they can be fooled or forgotten. Brett Weston, a master photographer with sixty-five years of experience says of the Zone System, "I don't use it. I don't have time for all those calculations and besides, what do you do if you lose your meter or it breaks?" His attitude reflects that of many intuitive workers, but no one can deny the fact that he understands the response of his materials to light and development. He does not express them in Zone System terms but neither does a sensitometrist.

Most students *cannot* use the Zone System without a light meter, but to say that no one can correctly estimate an exposure for a given zone placement is inaccurate. Even when we use a meter we constantly make adjustments for physical conditions and the limitations of our equipment, based on experience. The degree of experience that we apply to our technique and the accuracy that we require, determine our use of the light meter. *Use a light meter for accuracy and consistency,* but be careful when you assume that because you require one, everyone does.

The Zone System Eliminates the Need for Dodging and Burning Prints   The Zone System can reasonably predict one placed zone and one zone that we have targeted to base our development upon. This designates both ends of the scale, but what if we wish to change a tone in the middle of the scale? An efficient method of altering any local area is dodging and burning during printing. These tools can also compensate for human errors and imperfections in the materials or equipment which no system can eliminate. Dodging and burning are two of the most useful creative tools we possess and the Zone System is designed to extend control, not limit it.

Zone System Negatives Can All Be Printed on the Same Contrast Grades of Paper   If a film cannot plus or minus as much as the photographer needs, then the different contrast grades of paper offer the alternative that can tailor the print to suit creative needs. With roll film it may be the most practical solution to different scene contrasts, and the use of different papers can still be discussed in Zone System terms. The idea of matching a negative to a specific paper grade is to provide a solid basis for technique, not to limit creative choice. Another important aspect of controlling development is to promote practice and accuracy in visualization.

The Zone System Eliminates the Need to "Bracket" Exposures
"Bracketing" means making several negatives at different exposures to insure getting one good one. The reality is that photographers make as many negatives as they feel are necessary to insure the success of the photograph. Some are proud that they make only one exposure and some, like me, make several if they feel it is necessary. Either way, it makes small difference to the viewer. Aside from bracketing for exposure it may be necessary to make several negatives for a number of reasons: moving subjects in the scene such as water or clouds, changing lighting, dust spots on the film, equipment problems, etc. These are all valid reasons to make several exposures. I submit that making several negatives is not a confession of technical incompetence. It shows an understanding of a less than perfect system and a commitment to the work. I suggest an alternative for the term "bracket" for those photographers who wish to avoid the issue. My facetious term for bracketing is "variable zone placement." We place a subject on a zone, make a negative and then make another negative placing the subject one zone higher. Variable zone placement sounds very professional and the whole notion that we should not use this very simple "insurance," *when needed,* (I don't advocate wasting film!) is a matter of ego, not craft.

Photography is not an exact science and no method proves this more quickly than the Zone System. Don't throw away any procedures that help insure good work.

The Zone System Is a Difficult and Exotic Process   When chromo- genic film (a film using dyes instead of silver to form the final image) was introduced, one ad proclaimed, "From this moment on, the Zone System is dead." I fear this is a common attitude toward the Zone System. Somehow the simple craft of photography has become entangled with philosophy and mysticism. The "Zone System is dead" statement says if the method of control is changed then the entire concept of communication is negated.

MW 17

Photographer Minor White often joked that he used the "Zen System" of photography. This statement reflects his personal attitude about *applying* his craft, not the literal control the Zone System offers.

If chromogenic films produce gray tones in a print, then control of these tones can be related in Zone System terms. It may respond to development differently, it may respond to exposure differently, but its control proce- dures can be communicated.

If a tree is described as being zone V value, it could be referring to a photograph, a lithograph, a charcoal sketch, or a reproduction in a maga- zine. In each case the process for getting the zone V tone is different but in all cases the reader has a clear, visual reference of what a zone V tone is. The Zone System is not a reinvention of the photographic process; it is just a way to teach craft with literal, visual references. Any photographer who has tried to communicate via gammas, contrast index charts, density ranges, and characteristic curves has found the Zone System is another way of communicating craft—not the best way, not the worst. It is not the pur- pose of this text to dispute any methods of communication that work. The Zone System is one way many photographers find simple and functional.

MW 9

The Zone System Produces Good Negatives Every Time   The idea the Zone System will solve all your photographic problems is absurd. This also applies to any methodology and equipment regardless of claims made by manufacturers or devotees of specific procedures. The Zone System, when used with insight and care, makes a practical mastery of the pho- tographic process possible. It cannot eliminate human error or the imper- fections of photographic materials and it does have its limits in the creative sense. Even if it doesn't produce perfect negatives, it does help to increase negative consistency. It also offers a method to visually and technically assess problems and suggest some direction in which a solution may be found.

The Zone System Is the Same Thing as Sensitometry   This idea is the most highly debated of the Zone System myths and is actually a half truth. Many photographers who have never used a densitometer and do not use sensitometric terms use the Zone System. The fact that purely visual testing is possible is confirmation of this.

The Zone System *is* sensitometry in that it uses light sensitive materials and must follow all of the physical rules that govern their use.

Sensitometry is a science and the Zone System is one way to use that science to think about and control practical photography. In a very real sense the Zone System is a "rounding off" of the numbers used in sensitometry.

As soon as we assign a density number to a zone we have no alternative but to apply a disclaimer that the number represents only the midpoint of the zone. The concept of zones is based on the idea that a general density range that produces a general tone is more important than any specific density in itself. It is not as technically accurate as pure sensitometry but it was not designed to be. It sets a visual goal which can be achieved by technical measurement or by a trial and error approach. The degree of accuracy that you require is up to you.

STANDARDS
Precision and Practicality
Remarkably, the technical standards of the photographic process differ from manufacturer to manufacturer and sometimes even from country to country. This includes film speed determination, paper grading, light meter calibration and even cultural definitions of what a good print is. This is not to say the variations are wildly divergent to the point of chaos. It is a cautionary note to the reader to realize some latitude exists in defining technical limits.

The greatest conflict with these discrepancies lies not in the manufacturer's differences but in the failure of the photographer to investigate the reasons for these differences.

One of the first assumptions that many Zone System workers make is that the manufacturer's technical information is incorrect because the film speed and/or development time does not match the results of their own tests. This is usually done with no understanding of the limitations placed on precise, technical information.

By presenting a description of some of the thinking behind technical standards it is hoped that some of the theoretical vs. practicality conflicts can be understood. No specific products or brand names are targeted.

The basis for determining film speed and normal development time are interrelated. The amount of development affects the film's response to light and the development time is determined by how much of a brightness difference should be recorded as detailed values. In Zone System terms: How many zones should be recorded with detail on a grade #2 paper? If we wish to represent zone III and zone VII as *fully* detailed values, the development time is different than if we intend to make the detailed range zone III to zone IX. If the development time changes, the measurable film speed is different.

 MW 12

The film speed is based on the zone I value and it moves very slightly. In most cases this movement is not important in a practical sense, but in the strict technical sense it must be taken into account.

Part of technical accuracy is dependent upon the precision of the measuring devices. If they measure very fine increments even the smallest deviation from the designated goal must be considered inaccurate.

The manufacturer's differences are not as extreme as the example. They are often so close as to be measured in hundredths of a zone or less. The lesson here is that the most precise data and testing in the world will not match another photographer's results if the reference points are not the same. The same film and developer combination tested by two different manufacturers will probably yield two different film speeds and different normal development times.

Another aspect of technical standards is that they do not necessarily have anything to do with how a photograph *looks*. The visual references of the Zone System are based on normal development producing a scale of grays that look a certain way, that have a certain visual relationship.

The normal development given by a manufacturer may have little to do with the appearance of a photograph. It is a standard time that meets several precise technical criteria that do not necessarily reflect what we consider to be a normal looking gray scale in a print. This standard time determines film speed and accounts for some of the differences between the ISO speed and the working film speed for the Zone System.

As these differences carry over to the formulation of developers and the production of printing papers it causes a kind of domino effect. Each step of the process creates a small change in the product which in the end can become important enough to see visually. This is partially responsible for the inconsistency in the grading of photographic papers; they are the end product of this chain of events and we can see the difference here.

One more reason the manufacturer's standards should be explored is their ability to measure changes exceeds that of all but the most dedicated amateurs. With greater precision comes the ability to predict very minute variations and this is of major importance in scientific method. When the film speed or development is measured with the precision of laboratory equipment the changes take on a significance that is important but not within our ability to detect by visual means. This provides information we cannot determine for ourselves.

The 18% Gray Card

The concept of the 18% gray card as representing a "medium" gray tone has obscure roots. This is a tone that reflects 18% of the light that falls on it. If logic tells you that halfway between 0% of the light and 100% of the light is 50%, part of the confusion is obvious. Actually a tone of 50% reflectance looks like a very light gray value approximating a zone VII ½ tone. This is hardly a visual medium gray.

One explanation for this particular reflectance value is it conforms to the graphic artist's medium gray tone for the average subject that is copied for reproduction. It is the center point of the graphic arts gray scale and an appropriate measuring target for copying.

Another possible origin of the 18% standard involves a very subjective approach. When cards of various reflectances are shown to a number of viewers the reflectances selected as a "medium" gray tone fall into a fairly narrow range between 15% to 25% reflectance.

The suggestion is that 18% is approximately one half of the reflectance of the average Caucasian skin (36% reflectance) and it falls very close to the center of the range of the visual medium gray. If we meter an 18% gray card and place it on zone V, a Caucasian skin tone will automatically fall on zone VI which is where it is often placed.

As far as the Zone System is concerned any specific reference point could be used and it is fortunate this particular standard is one of the few points most photographic information sources agree upon.

One point must be made clear; although the 18% gray card was intended as a light metering target, it does not necessarily represent the middle reflectance of any particular scene. It is a target of known characteristics and offers a consistent reference tone. The assumption that it is *the* middle gray of a scene is erroneous in many circumstances and to use it in that manner can cause exposure problems. Understanding the source of the gray card helps us to use it correctly or to modify the information in an intelligent way.

Light Meter Calibration

Most light meters are calibrated to the specifications of the American National Standards Institute (ANSI). This determines the zone value the meter will place. ANSI calibrations do not consider zone I as a usable minimum zone. The meters are set up using a value of about zone I ½ as the lowest minimum usable zone. It places values slightly below zone V not because it is malfunctioning but because it uses a slightly different reference point. This point corresponds approximately to the midpoint of the usable scale of color films but may cause a slight underexposure for black and white films.

The solution for Zone System workers is to lower the film speed we set on the meter dial. This, when combined with the way film speeds are determined by the manufacturer, is a major cause of the lower meter setting usually encountered in Zone System testing. One problem students have is they think the meter setting somehow affects the film's sensitivity to light. They think if we lower the meter setting for the Zone System, then the Zone System must be very inefficient because it makes the film response to light so much lower. Actually, we are adjusting the meter to give us information that is different than it is designed to give. Other systems have claimed to be more efficient because the meter can be set at higher film speeds, but they do not use the meter in the same manner or use the same gray scale relationships. We could set the meter at 400 for a film rated at 50, but we could also assume it places a zone II value and open up 3 f-stops for a zone V reading. The *use* of the meter is more important than the literal speed setting. Some camera metering *systems*, although calibrated to ANSI standards, will give different effective zone placements depending upon the scene. Only if the subject is evenly toned and lighted will they respond like more conventional meters. They make several readings and integrate them in uneven proportions.

CHAPTER 6 SUMMARY
Myths

As with many aspects of photography, myths will persist about the Zone System. Most involve the difficulty of separating the craft itself from the application of the craft. The Zone System does not reinvent photography, it redefines some of the terms and provides an atmosphere for learning the practical use of the technology. Ansel Adams once said, "It (the Zone System) does cause some debate but it also works as a step toward understanding the concepts of sensitometry on a practical level."

Standards

The technical basis for processes and/or equipment may have little to do with how a photograph looks. Some technical standards are limited by the need for scientific accuracy. The precision of measuring instruments makes even very small deviations inaccurate because the result is so specifically defined.

Different manufacturers may have different standards upon which their technical information is based. Technical discrepancies may be small in themselves but they have a cumulative effect that may be significant.

It is important for a photographer to investigate the basis for technical information before assuming that testing information is right or wrong.

CHAPTER 7   The Monkey Wrench

he title of this chapter refers to the things that make any process
more difficult—the many imperfections and details that become obvious as theory is put into practice. This is the wrench that falls into
the machinery and jams it. It is intended as a reference chapter, and it is
strongly advised that you read the main text thoroughly and clear up any
concept problems before using this chapter. The Zone System has been
presented in its simplest form to help the reader understand its basic forms
and limits without the complications of minutia. No ideas from the main
text are contradicted; they are clarified and detailed to reveal the practical
boundaries of the system. Other areas of photography that directly relate
to exposure and development are included to various degrees.

Sections containing procedures for specific methods or materials are
designated MW-P.

ZONE SIZE

If you examined the zone scale of grays carefully you may have noticed
the stepping of tones is not even. Films distort the recording of brightness
differences. The way we have designated the zones reflects this distortion.

MW 1 Chapter 1,
page 3; also Chapter 5,
page 55

We have presented a series of definite gray steps. They are predictable
and repeatable but they are not evenly spaced. A bar graph, Figure 7.1,
illustrates the spacing differences. Like a staircase with steps of different
heights at the bottom and top of the scale, the photographic process does
not record a scene evenly. A doubling of brightness in the scene always
moves a value up one zone step on the scale, but the steps are not always
the same height.

In practice the differences look like this: if we measured each zone as
we would a staircase in a house, the size of each step would be different
in the extreme lows than in the middle and high zones. Zones III, II and
I are progressively smaller than zones VI, V and IV. Because they are smaller
they do not have as much room for the subtle changes in tone that make
up our "zone." If we divide the space between a zone V and a zone VI into
ten equal parts, the parts are large enough to easily distinguish between
them. Very subtle tone differences can be distinguished. If we divide the
space between a zone II and a zone III value into ten equal parts, the parts
are so small we cannot easily see them. The film cannot record the very

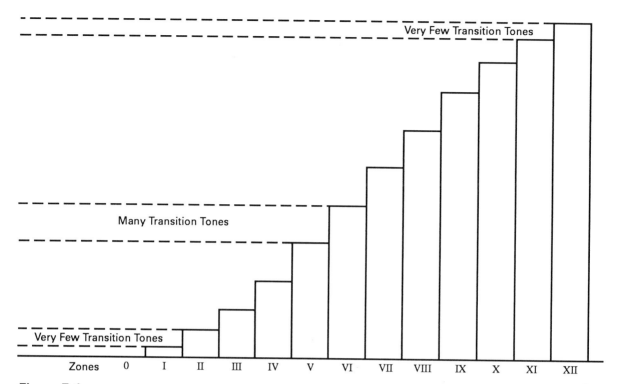

Figure 7.1 *Verbally, we have described gray scale relationships as moving "up" on the scale for a lighter tone and "down" for darker tones. An easy way to diagram this is to draw the scale as a staircase.*
   When the height of each step is measured we can see that there is literally more room for in-between tones in the middle of the gray scale than at either extreme. The transition from one zone to the next is more abrupt in the very low and very high zones. This means that the film records more subtle gradations of tone in the middle of the gray scale.

subtle brightness differences in the scene. The film is very inefficient in the low zones. If the film does not record the in-between tones we cannot print them.

It is like playing a piano that has keys missing in the first and last octaves of the keyboard. As long as we use the middle range of the piano we can play it normally. As soon as we use the extremes of the keyboard the music cannot be played without leaving some notes out. This distorts the music. The inability to see the in-between tones, the subtle shadings in the extreme zones, is an inherent part of the photographic process.

We could expose the film so much that none of the scene brightnesses fall on the low zones and then expose the negative onto the printing paper for a very long time. This means we would print a zone V exposure down to a zone II or III, but on some films the very high zones also distort in the same way as the lows. We would be trading the distortion in the lows for distortion in the highs. The extreme overexposure also increases grain, decreases sharpness, and can make printing times unreasonably long.

VARIATIONS IN LIGHT METER SYSTEMS

MW 2 Chapter 1, page 6

The ideal light meter is our model for Chapter 1, but meter responses can vary dramatically in practical use. Manufacturers attempt to compensate for a variety of picture-taking situations by adjusting their metering *systems* and the calibration of these systems. Factory adjusted meters can give exposure placements that range from zone IV to zone VI ½. Priorities differ with each manufacturer and they try to guess what kind of photograph you will make. This results in a diversity of ideas about what is the "correct" zone value. It is more important that the meter tells how to make the same zone value every time.

Some programmable systems can even shift the basic zone placement to accommodate the use of color transparency films whose "middle gray" is slightly darker than for negative films. This helps to avoid overexposure.

Light meters can read in-between zones such as zone V ¼ or zone VI ⅛, so don't be surprised if this happens and be willing to accept that it may not be possible to adjust "out" this ⅛ zone.

The basis of a zone V exposure is a formula including film speed, subject brightness as measured in candles per square foot, and a number of subjective ideas about what is the proper middle gray. This can be explored in various sensitometry books but does not greatly concern the working photographer. (See Chapter 6 and the meter calibration section in Chapter 8.)

If a meter reads a consistent zone VI instead of zone V we can still place values by starting at zone VI. Procedures for calibrating a light meter for the Zone System are included in the testing section.

RELATIONSHIP OF TIME, TEMPERATURE, DILUTION, AND AGITATION

Many aspects of developers affect contrast other than actual developing time. Temperature of the solution, agitation intervals and patterns, and developer composition (including dilution) may affect contrast.

MW 3 Chapter 2, page 12

If these aspects of development are thought of as checks and balances to each other, the basic relationships of the aspects can be examined. When one of these factors is *increased* (higher temperature, more development time, more agitation, or stronger developer), we generally get more contrast if all of the other factors remain the same.

Conversely, if one factor is *decreased* (lower temperature, less time, less agitation, or weaker developer), we get less contrast.

These aspects can be used to offset each other to maintain a balance of contrast. If the temperature of the developer is lowered, we can increase the development time, agitate more or increase the developer strength to compensate.

The useful limits of each control are different and must be tested. It may not be possible to fully correct one aspect by changing another.

I recommend that the student begin by changing only the development time for contrast control. All other factors should remain constant to avoid confusion. They will seldom limit contrast control. Extreme changes may be the exception and require that more than one aspect be altered.

NOTE: The most common causes of inaccurate development in school situations are usually incorrect temperature readings and/or weak or exhausted developer.

CONTRAST CHANGES USING EXPOSURE CONTROLS

There are several ways to alter contrast either directly or indirectly that involve exposure. Most, by their very nature, are difficult to control and predict but the creative worker should be aware of these possibilities. They deserve a book in themselves but will only be touched upon here. I urge the reader to find out more about these areas of exposure/contrast control.

MW 4 Chapter 2, page 16

Strong filtration can actually reverse zone relationships if the subject's color saturation is sufficient. A bright red object might be less reflective (darker) than a bright blue object and still record as a lighter tone if a strong red filter is used during exposure. (See Appendix for more on filters.)

When very long exposures (over 1 second) or very short exposures (1/1000 second or less) are made, the film does not react to light in its usual way because the amount of light reaching the film is so low. This reaction is called reciprocity departure, reciprocity failure or the reciprocity effect. (See Appendix.) A recommended exposure for a zone V value will be underexposed. All values will be recorded as lower zones than the meter indicates, and the lower the zone the more it will be underexposed. With the lows moving down more than the highs we get a contrast increase. The longer the exposure the larger the deviation. Very slow graphic arts films used this effect to increase contrast. Reliable charts are available to explain these effects.

Pre-exposure of the film can reduce contrast. The film is fogged very slightly before the scene is photographed. This supports the low zones by providing a kind of foundation of density but has almost no effect on the high zones. This lowers the effective difference between the zones. This method can be of use but extreme care must be taken and most photographers prefer to use other methods if possible. When used in the printing of photographs this is called "flashing" the paper and is useful in lowering paper contrast. Flashing is covered in detail in Phil Davis' text *Beyond the Zone System*. For information on pre-exposure, see appendix sections, "The Zone System and Color Films" and "The Zone System and Flash Photography."

It is possible to dodge and burn during negative exposure if the length of time permits. This is a contrast change through exposure but it is very difficult to be consistent. Polaroid films can be immensely helpful in providing immediate feedback about placement of dodging and burning tools.

POLAROID FILM TONAL SCALES

MW 5 Chapter 2, page 19

Polaroid materials have a shorter working scale than conventional films. Generally above zone VII ½ there is little or no discernable detail in the prints, and below approximately zone III no detail is visible. The type 52 sheet film will sometimes show texture as low as zone II in the print. Placements and visual judgments must be made with these limitations in mind. Polaroid materials are excellent when used within described limits. The scale can vary with different Polaroid film types.

Some Polaroid films will produce a high quality, sheet film negative (Type 55) which can be cleared in a sodium sulfite solution on location for immediate judgment and later printed by conventional means. It may require a slightly different exposure to produce an optimum negative than for a good print with this material. The working scale of the negative is also slightly longer than the print and must be considered when this film is used for testing.

Temperature differences will alter the speed and contrast of Polaroid films and when using them for outdoor demonstrations allowances should be made for their protection. All films are packaged with appropriate instructions for use.

These films are more than just useful for tests. They have unique visual qualities and are unparalleled for certain subjects and situations. More and more they are being used as preferred material for artists in both black and white and color. I urge the serious student to investigate these films and to consider them as a material equal to conventional films for creative work.

AVERAGE SCENE BRIGHTNESS RANGE

By measuring many scenes with a light meter we could determine an average brightness range and ultimately come up with an "average" scene. A long accepted average is a scene that measures a brightness difference of 160:1.

MW 6 Chapter 3, page 21

Since each zone reflects twice the light of the previous zone, the amount of light doubles with every zone we move up on the scale. This means that the light ratio progresses geometrically. A one f-stop difference means a 2:1 ratio, a two f-stop difference a 4:1 ratio, a three f-stop difference an 8:1 ratio, and so on.

This works out to an "average" scene having about a 7 ½ zone difference that should be recorded with some kind of tone (zones I–VIII). When we add the accent tones of zone 0 and zone IX the total becomes a 9 ½ f-stop difference. It is obvious that the Zone System scale is not only convenient but also a product of observation and measurement. It is also consistent with Zone System philosophy to "round off" the 9 ½ tone scale to 10 zones to facilitate visualization.

A 160:1 average is only an average of all the scenes measured. Most of the scenes you encounter will not measure exactly 160:1.

Throughout the history of photography this type of averaging has been influential in setting technical standards. This includes ideas about how a photograph *should* look. It is not surprising, considering how much opinion is involved, that there are disputes over what is a normal scale of tones. Major technical disputes can sometimes be traced to differing opinions of what a good print is supposed to look like.

LOW ZONE MOVEMENT AND EXPOSURE COMPENSATIONS

No system is perfect and the lower zones do move with development changes. The movement is slight but it can be measured visually and sensitometrically. With some films a zone III value can be moved upward as much as ¾ zone with extended development. More significant is the downward movement resulting from minus developments. The low zones are at the minimum point needed to produce an image. They have received the least amount of exposure necessary to create their tones, and even a minus one (N–1) development may be enough to weaken these low values. Development reduction may produce a less brilliant quality to the lows and care must be taken to avoid loss of detail. Special agitation methods can be used and exposure modifications can compensate to reduce the loss of low value quality due to this movement. Chapter 5 covers some of the processing methods that help reduce these problems. A specific test for low zone movement can be found in the testing section.

MW 7 Chapter 3, page 22

CONTRAST POTENTIAL

MW 8 *Chapter 3, page 23, also Chapter 5, page 54*

In general the higher speed films (above ISO 100) tend to reduce in contrast very readily. Efficient reduction of more than one zone (N–1) is usually not accomplished just by reducing the development time. Alterations in development methods, including agitation changes, are often necessary to avoid serious weakening of the low values. Beware of shortcuts in testing procedures since it is possible to make a high zone move downward the correct amount but it is essential to check the movement of the lows. Small changes in density in the low zones make dramatic quality changes. Exposure increases are usually required in addition to reduced development. Some of these special considerations are discussed in Chapter 5.

Films of ISO 100 or less are more likely to increase in contrast more easily than the faster films. Expansion beyond (N+1) is usually possible with an appropriate reduction in exposure to compensate for the upward movement of the low values. Special developers may be used but increased grain size can become a factor even with large format negatives. To achieve expansions of N+3 or more it is possible to substitute a high contrast film such as Kodak Technical Pan or graphic arts films instead of using development increases. (See the Materials and Processes chapter for a detailed description.)

The new tabular grained films from Kodak and Ilford exhibit an unusually wide range of contrasts. Even the faster speed films will expand to an N+2 contrast increase but they require a higher degree of processing precision than conventional films. MW #18 has a more detailed description of their characteristics.

SENSITOMETRIC TERMS DESCRIBING CONTRAST

MW 9 *Chapter 6, page 65*

Gamma, average gradient, contrast index and density ranges are all sensitometric terms which describe the contrast of photo sensitive materials. Each explains contrast based on a slightly different set of priorities and each describes tone relationships using numerical or graphic means.

Gamma refers only to the straight line section of the film's characteristic curve (see sensitometry section, Chapter 8, Section 2) and does not include the extreme low values (zones I–III) in its measurements. Occasionally values as high as zone IV are not measured. Because it does not include these important low values, gamma is seldom used in modern literature when describing contrast. Gamma also does not measure the extreme high values that fall on the shoulder of the film's curve.

Generally, if a gamma value is less than one it means the contrast of the material is less than normal. A number higher than one indicates a greater than normal contrast.

The *average gradient* method selects two points on the characteristic curve, a low and a high value density, and a straight line is drawn between them. The line is assigned a decimal number depending upon its angle. The higher the number the steeper the angle and the greater the contrast. A normal contrast negative is approximately a value of .50 to .60.

Contrast index is a special form of average gradient used by the Eastman Kodak Company. It is plotted in basically the same manner but the two reference points are different. This results in a slightly different numbering. Normal contrast is usually assigned a contrast index number of about .56, and the higher the number the higher the contrast.

Both the average gradient and the contrast index numbering method include virtually the entire zone scale and are much more appropriate than gamma in describing the zones that are actually used to produce a photograph. (See Figure 7.2.)

A *density range* describes the difference between any two points on the characteristic curve. Two values are measured by a densitometer and the low number is subtracted from the high number. The result is the difference between the densities called the density range. The higher the number the greater the contrast difference. Table MW-1 shows how the density range describes these differences.

Density range numbers may be used to describe all or part of a film or paper tonal range.

The complex applications and backgrounds of these terms cannot be adequately discussed in the confines of this text. The reader should refer to one of the many descriptions offered in other photographic references to obtain further information. The excellent text *Beyond the Zone System*, by Phil Davis, offers an extensive look at the science of sensitometry.

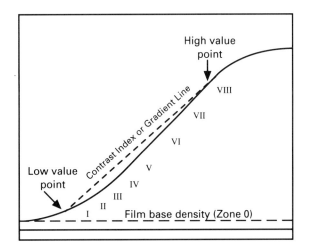

Figure 7.2 *Average gradient and contrast index numbers refer to the angle of a straight line drawn between two selected points on a film's characteristic curve. Each method of contrast description uses slightly different reference points on the curve.*

The angle of the straight section of the curve is used as the measurement for gamma. In this sample, values below approximately zone IV and above approximately zone VIII would not be measured by gamma designations. The zone values shown do not refer to a specific film.

TABLE MW-1

High density (zone VIII)	1.35	*This DR describes a moderate contrast negative.*
Low density (zone III)	.35	
Density range	1.00	
High density (zone X)	1.75	*This DR describes a high contrast negative.*
Low density (zone III)	.35	
Density range	1.40	

CORRECT EXPOSURE AND THE MINIMUM DENSITY NEGATIVE

MW 10 *Chapter 3,*
page 25

The sensitometric definition of "correct" exposure is the negative that has the *least* light stopping power (density) that will still produce the desired results. It reduces to the statement: Don't waste light; don't give anymore exposure than is really necessary.

In order to maintain this minimum density it is theoretically necessary to adjust our exposure *whenever* we deviate from the normal development time. *Every* development change causes a change in the effective film speed. If we give a plus development we must reduce the working speed of the film (give less exposure) or we will not produce a minimum density negative. If we minus the film we must increase the exposure to compensate for the downward movement of the low zones.

The advantages of a minimum density negative include:

1. The maximum working film speed.
2. The sharpest possible negative, all other things being equal.
3. The minimum exposure time needed for printing.

While all of these qualities are desirable, it is necessary to put the information into a practical perspective. If we fail to make exposure compensations for low zone movement, the practical effect may not be serious enough to visually affect the final print.

Plus development increases all densities. The low zone increase is very slight, but in the definition of a minimum density negative some exposure compensation is needed to insure the densities are kept to a minimum. Since it is assumed the negative required a plus development by choice, any increase in grain due to increased development cannot be counted. What can be adjusted is the literal density that results from the slightly higher working film speed. The zone I value has moved upward slightly and we base our film speed on the zone I value. If it moves up, the film speed has effectively increased. We can adjust the exposure to keep our low zones at the minimum level. We are discussing the slight difference in density produced by the exposure, *not* the plus development since we have decided a plus development was needed to interpret the scene correctly anyway.

If we do not compensate for the upward movement:

1. We produce slightly grainier negatives. This excess grain is not noticeable in practical work unless carried to extreme development increases.
2. The negative sharpness is decreased very slightly unless overexposure is carried to the extreme. Most negatives are not noticeably less sharp at normal print sizes.
3. Longer printing times are needed and this can become a problem if the density of the negative is extreme. This increases the possibility of enlarger movement and reciprocity failure of the paper.

When the development is less than normal the results are more serious. The low zones are already at a minimum and if exposure compensations are not made, they fall below the minimum level needed to produce their tone or they may disappear altogether. If we make even a slight error on the side of underexposure and then compound it by failing to increase exposure for the minus development the results can be disastrous. The lower the zone the smaller the margin for error.

A basic guideline is to decrease the exposure ⅓ f-stop for every full zone you move upward. A plus one development would require a ⅓ f-stop decrease from the exposure calculated by meter. A plus two development would need a ⅔ f-stop decrease.

For the minus developments increase the exposure ½ f-stop for every full zone movement. A minus one development requires a ½ f-stop increase; a minus two requires a one full f-stop increase in the calculated exposure.

This is compensation on the side of overexposure but the consequences of a slightly overexposed negative are much less severe than underexposure of black and white negatives.

These compensations are not a substitute for proper testing. They are general guidelines for many films. Greater accuracy can only be accomplished with careful testing either through experience or scientific method.

A method of determining low zone movement and exposure compensations is outlined in the testing section.

DILUTING DEVELOPERS FOR CONTRAST CONTROL

Diluting developers for contrast control is one of the least understood of all photographic processes. The subject is complex but let it suffice to say that diluting a developer does not in itself reduce contrast in a negative or print unless it is diluted so much that there is not enough chemistry to develop the material.

MW 11 Chapter 5, page 57

Most contrast reduction occurs because when the developer is diluted, the time necessary to reach normal development is increased. If the normal time (undiluted) is 5 minutes then the diluted formula may require 8 minutes to produce normal contrast. If the film is still developed for only 5 minutes, the film has been given less development than normal which is the definition of a minus development.

Dilution changes *combined* with intelligent agitation pattern changes can reduce contrast significantly even with standard developers but greater than normal exposures are usually needed. See Chapter 5 for some of the practical applications.

It is important to remember that when developer is diluted to increase working time, it may exhaust if the agitation interval is too long. This means that the more we dilute a developer the more frequent the agitation must be to avoid disproportionate development.

Do not be fooled by the failure of the dilute developer to produce normal results even with extreme time increases. It may be exhausted due to excessive dilution. Exhausted developer *will* produce less contrast.

An old method of determining print development was called development by factor and illustrates how dilution affects the time needed to reach any specific contrast. During development the appearance of a specific gray tone is timed (usually zone V). The time it takes for this tone to appear is noted and the print is developed 6X to 8X the noted time, i.e., if the zone V tone appears in 15 seconds and the print is developed for 2 minutes, we have a ratio of 1:8. If a print with the same exposure was placed in the same developer but at an unknown dilution, we could time the appearance of the zone V tone, multiply by 8 and produce virtually an identical print. The dilution must not be so severe as to exhaust the developer, and prolonged safelight exposure must be avoided.

With any developer a point is reached where it will no longer produce maximum density in film or paper. Most photographers will avoid this effect for aesthetic reasons. This is a reduction in contrast but not a very usable one.

The contention that dilution gives finer grain is also suspicious. It may be the indirect result of using the dilute developer for lessening contrast. If the film is given minus development it *is* less grainy. We generally don't dilute developers for plus development.

Diluting a developer does not increase the amount of film that can be developed. The total amount of film that can be developed remains the same despite the increased volume of solution.

NOTE: In the scientific community a dilution using a colon such as 1:2 means that the final dilution should contain a *total* of *two parts* and a 1:2 dilution really means equal parts of each solution are used. To avoid confusion, I use the designation 1+2 to mean one part of one solution plus two parts of another solution to make a *total* of three parts. Highly technical sources concerning chemistry may use either designation and the difference is important. The higher the dilution the less important this distinction becomes.

TECHNICAL DETERMINATION OF FILM SPEED

MW 12   *Chapter 6,*
page 66

For those who are interested in the purely technical data for determining film speed: the film speed is the result of exposing the film to produce a film density of .1 above the film base plus fog density when the film is developed so that a brightness range of 1.3 in the scene produces a density range of .8 in the negative. The .1 density is called the speed point when it is used as a reference. Any density can be referred to as a speed point if it is used as a reference point.

The Zone System uses a density value of .1 above film base plus fog for a zone I value when the film is developed to record a textured range of zone II to zone VIII from a scene brightness range of seven f-stops.

The numbers used in the sensitometric measurement of film densities are logarithmic. They are used to relate the scene brightnesses to exposure and development results. An introduction to the science of sensitometry can be found in Chapter 8, Section 2.

The Zone System standard and the sensitometric standard are not precisely the same, and in most cases the film speed on the meter must be lowered to produce the Zone System gray scale.

VARIABLE CONTRAST PAPERS

MW 13   *Chapter 5,*
page 53

Variable contrast papers are sensitive to both blue and green light. Using filters or enlarging light sources changes the ratio of blue to green light, which changes the amount of contrast in the print.

The example in Table MW–2 shows a generic manufacturer's recommendations for the use of dichroic color head filtration for contrast variations. Each paper brand requires a different filtration depending on the

TABLE MW–2

Paper grade	Dichroic head filtration (½ grades can be inferred)
0	110 yellow
1	70 yellow
2	no filtration
3	45 magenta
4	95 magenta
5	170 magenta

light source used. Most manufacturers publish color head recommendations for their papers. The alternative is to purchase the special filters designed for use with most black and white enlarger heads.

In this example, blue light from the enlarger is absorbed by the yellow filtration and the contrast is decreased. The less blue light that reaches the paper the lower the contrast.

When magenta filtration is added, the contrast of the paper is increased. The magenta filtration absorbs green light so the less green light that reaches the paper the higher the contrast.

The paper requires no filtration to produce normal contrast since it is designed to respond normally to certain enlarging light sources. These sources are not always specified but the information usually applies to tungsten enlarging lamps.

If the filter information is given for tungsten lamps it does not apply to some cold light enlarging lamps. (See Appendix.) The blue to green proportions of gaseous tube lamps are not standardized. The proper cold light tube must be used for accurate grading or the tube must be filtered *in addition to* the recommended filtration. Most cold light heads designed for variable contrast papers are clearly specified by the manufacturer. Be certain that the safelight that you use is designed for variable contrast papers.

The general trend of cold light heads is to produce excessive amounts of blue light. On most papers this results in too much contrast. There are special heads manufactured by the Ilford and Oriental Photo companies that are designed to print on variable contrast papers by varying the color of the enlarging light. This light source is not designed for printing color photographs but is useful if large numbers of prints on variable contrast papers are being produced. The dichroic color heads are more flexible since they will work with variable contrast papers and can also be used for color printing.

Some developers such as pyrogallic acid (pyro) stain negatives a brownish yellow color and this stain acts as a contrast filter on VC papers. Testing is necessary to determine the actual contrast grading for these developers and staining will differ with age, amount of development, and the film and developer combination.

RECIPROCITY FAILURE OF PRINTING PAPERS

MW 14 *Chapter 5,*
page 54

As with all conventional photographic emulsions, printing papers exhibit reciprocity failure when the light intensity is very low. The effect of increased contrast is similar to films but the values affected are reversed. The threshold values (the areas with the least amounts of silver image) are the high values. This is where the reciprocity failure is most pronounced and will occur first.

It is important to think of effects such as reciprocity failure as a *characteristic* of the paper and not as always a problem. It is possible to use this effect to change the contrast response of the paper to our advantage. We may desire more contrast from the paper and the effect then becomes an asset. (See Appendix for more detailed information.)

Reciprocity failure in papers can be observed by making a simple test. Expose a Kodak step tablet at a relatively short printing exposure (about 20–30 seconds) and adjust the light intensity to produce a full range of tones to include a pure black and pure white tone. Develop the print normally.

Repeat the test but adjust the exposure time to exceed 1–2 minutes and print to match a relatively light tone (about zone VII). Develop the second print normally and compare it to the first. The number of steps with tone should be slightly different if the paper is exhibiting reciprocity failure. This shows as a contrast increase. The difference may be subtle unless the light intensity is decreased drastically.

"CONTRAST" AS A VARIABLE TERM

MW 15 *Chapter 3,*
page 22

In photography the word "contrast" is used in so many ways that a single definition is not possible. Sensitometrically the word generally implies the difference between densities or values by defining the space between them. A larger difference, either mathematically or visually, indicates more contrast. The density difference between a density of .25 and 1.25 is larger than the difference between .25 and .35 so the contrast is greater.

While this definition applies to many technical aspects of assessing photographic prints, the more common use of the word implies something different. When viewing prints we tend to express contrast from an emotional point of view and are usually referring to the number of gray tones in the photograph.

If a print contains only two values, pure black and pure white, we call it a high contrast print. Another print may contain the same pure black and white values but if it also has many intermediate tones we refer to it as a lower contrast print. The total number of different tones becomes the basis for our judgment.

These differences in usage are not contradictory but they do reflect a difference in priorities as well as the human tendency to respond emotionally to the final print. Either definition can be defended based on its ultimate application.

Photographic terms often contain this ambiguity and the Zone System offers only a tiny step toward clarifying the mixture of technique and aesthetics that make up creative photography.

It is for the student to actively question the terminology so that priorities can be explained and communication improved. Many terms are not
really misused as much as they are used to explain an undefined set of
effects.

D-MIN, D-MAX, AND DENSITY RANGES
OF PRINTING PAPERS

Manufacturers may list reflection densities for their papers. The listings
include a white reading and a pure black reading. The white reading is
abbreviated D-minimum and it refers to the minimum density of the image,
which is the white paper base. The black reading is the D-maximum and
refers to the maximum density of silver image, the blackest black that the
paper can produce.

MW 16 Chapter 5,
page 51

The readings are made with a reflection densitometer which measures
the light reflected from the print area and gives us a decimal number (see
Chapter 8). A small number means a very light tone because it is measuring
the density of the image, and a small image density lets a lot of the white
paper show through.

A paper might read a maximum white density of .06 and a maximum
black density of 2.15. These are the real densities for Oriental, Seagull G
papers.

Some papers may measure whiter whites and blacker blacks than other
papers but may visually appear the same. Tonal differences that seem significant mathematically are often impossible to detect when looking at
prints.

Literal density values are used as marketing information and are often
the only information given for papers. Too many other factors affect overall
print appearance to rely entirely on literal density values. Print color and
viewing light have substantial effects on print character and a warm tone
black may measure darker than a cold tone black and yet "feel" lighter in
value. D-minimum measurements may not include the visual effects of special paper whiteners called optical brighteners.

Direct comparison of print papers with the accompanying density value
information allows the photographer to translate the density values into
visual terms.

Contrast differences in papers are expressed in density range numbers.
This is sometimes called the exposure range or contrast range. A range of
1.70 is lower in contrast than a range of .65. The higher the numbers the
lower the contrast grade of the paper because the numbers express the *difference* between the two most extreme tones that it can reproduce. A large
density range number means that it will reproduce a large density difference in a negative (a very contrasty negative) as a normal looking print. A
small number indicates that a small density difference in the negative (a
low contrast negative) will reproduce as a normal looking print.

Common density range numbers for different contrast grades of paper
are listed in Table MW–3. These represent no specific paper brand.

TABLE MW–3

Paper grade	Density range (approx.)	Number of negative zones the paper will reproduce with detail
0	1.40–1.70	9 zone range (approx.)
1	1.16–1.39	8 zone range "
2	0.94–1.15	7 zone range "
3	0.80–0.93	6 zone range "
4	0.65–0.79	5 zone range "
5	0.50–0.64	4 zone range "

CHROMOGENIC FILMS

MW 17   *Chapter 6, page 65*

Chromogenic film is essentially a color film designed to make black and white negatives. It is processed using standard color negative chemistry (process C–41), and the image is formed with neutral colored dyes instead of silver particles.

The two major aspects of using this film are: it can be processed in any standard C–41 processor including the popular one-hour mini-labs, and it usually produces a finer grained image than conventional films of equal speed. The finer "grain" is actually composed of tiny dye globules which tend to be smaller than the clumps of normal silver grains.

Since chromogenic film has more than one emulsion like color film, the development is crucial. Each emulsion responds to development changes differently and it is only in a very narrow range that the emulsions coincide to make a relatively predictable image. Altering the development causes unusual color responses and contrast shifts so it is not recommended. Changing the grade of printing paper is the easiest way to alter image contrast.

It is possible to change contrast by giving more or less than the optimum exposure but the controls are limited. More than normal exposure will reduce contrast because the density of the high values is restricted by the addition of special developer inhibitors. Less than normal exposure does increase contrast but it is at the expense of low value detail. Contrast changes by this method are restricted to less than a plus or minus 1 change.

In the older chromogenic films some dye colors were not truly neutral and acted as contrast filters when printing on variable contrast paper. This altered the paper's response and contrast grading was not normal. The most recent film has a corrected dye balance for variable contrast papers.

The film also has an extended red sensitivity and red objects will photograph lighter than with conventional films. This may affect your use of filtration on the camera.

Chromogenic film is produced by the Ilford Corporation and is available in sheet, roll, and 35mm sizes.

TABULAR GRAIN FILMS (KODAK T-MAX 100 AND 400 AND ILFORD DELTA FILMS)

Because of their unique qualities, the T-Max films have been separated from the main text and detailed here.

MW 18 *Chapter 5, page 54*

The Tabular grained films developed by the Eastman Kodak Company use a differently shaped grain structure to provide a higher film speed with finer grain than conventional films.

In their requirements of precision of handling, these films deserve the name "Professional," and the student may find consistent results difficult to obtain unless processing procedures are consistent and developer recommendations made by the manufacturer are followed carefully.

The films can be developed in standard developers such as D–76 or HC–110 but the special T-Max developers are *strongly recommended* for consistency and quality of results when using these films.

Kodak calls this film "agitation sensitive" and I agree. The amount and method of agitation substantially affects the final image characteristics and should be carefully monitored. Specific recommendations for agitation are included in packaged film instructions. Some of the disproportionate development procedures may require modification to avoid uneven development. Contrast changes also occur rather rapidly and development times should be precise.

Recommended development temperatures are higher than normal (Kodak recommends 75 degrees F), and you will find that fixing the films not only takes longer but also uses up your fixer at a faster rate.

A special dye layer may present a pinkish cast if fixation is incomplete but its presence becomes a problem only if it is uneven. Re-fixing will usually clear this and I have found that an immersion in a hypo clearing agent often removes the pinkish color almost immediately.

Kodak recommends giving increased exposure (a vague one–two f-stops) for high contrast scenes and processing normally. This is a type of "variable zone placement" (see Chapter 6) and must be used with care and only when the T-Max developers are used. When some conventional developers are used the extreme high values produced by this overexposure will "shoulder" very quickly. This results in decreased contrast in the very high values which can be seen in the final print. I again stress the need to use the special developers designed for this film to achieve the maximum benefits from it.

The films change contrast readily and a development time increase will give an N+2 contrast even with the faster (ISO 400) film. With less-than-normal development times the contrast decreases rapidly and minus developments require careful timing. These films are among the most versatile in terms of contrast changing potential *when used with the T-Max developers.*

The negatives may *appear* slightly thinner (underexposed) than regular films and still print with normal contrast so don't attempt to judge quality without printing them.

The T-grain films also have very similar responses to daylight and tungsten light and do not require separate testing.

A variation on the tabular grain technology has been introduced by the Ilford Photo Corporation with their Delta films. The major advantage of the tabular shaped grain (from both manufacturers) is that it "flattens" the grain particle, providing a larger light gathering area. This gives increased light sensitivity with a relatively small grain size.

Delta film construction, called core-shell crystal technology, allows the use of less sensitizing dye than the T-Max films (which is the pinkish cast seen in the T-Max films) allowing the Delta emulsion to react more favorably to conventional developer formulas. The specialized T-grain developers are not necessary for the Delta films.

The Delta films reciprocity failure characteristics are similar to those of conventional films and the T-Max reciprocity charts *do not apply*. Fixing times for the Delta films will be longer than for conventional films and the manufacturer's agitation recommendations should be followed until careful, personal tests can be made.

PROCEDURE AND FORMULA FOR USING TWO-SOLUTION DEVELOPER

MW-P 19 *Chapter 5,*
page 56

This formula is used to control contrast with roll films. The low zones receive a relatively normal development and the high zones are limited in density. It is a variation of the water-bath process described in Chapter 5.

Solution 1   This is the Kodak D–23 formula.

Water at 125 degrees F	750.0 cc
Metol	7.5 g
Sodium Sulphite	100.0 g
Water to make	1000.0 cc

Solution 2

Water at 125 degrees F	100.0 cc
Borax (granular)	20.0 g
Water to make	1000.0 cc

The contrast is primarily determined by the time the film is in the first bath. The longer the time the greater the contrast.

The film is agitated constantly in the first solution and then transferred to the second solution *without draining*. I recommend that roll film users try to scale their negatives to an N–1 or N–1 ½ development for general high contrast scenes. Any greater contrast reductions can be achieved using paper grades. If greater reductions in contrast are required it is possible to achieve reductions of N–2 and N–3, but if any normal contrast scenes are included on the roll they may be reduced beyond a usable point. Exposure increases are usually needed beyond N–1.

A basic development plan for first tests is:

	Solution 1	**Solution 2**
N-1	6 minutes @ 68 degrees F	3 minutes @ 68 degrees F
	Solution 1	**Solution 2**
N-2	4 minutes @ 68 degrees F	3 minutes @ 68 degrees F

It has been suggested by Adams that after 15 seconds in solution 2 the film reel should be inverted and then left without agitation for the remainder of the 3 minutes. This is to avoid streaking due to chemical migration toward the bottom of the tank. In all cases the film should be left *without any agitation* unless streaking occurs.

Some experimentation has been done with much stronger alkaline solutions as a second bath. The suggestion is if the development is speeded up in the second bath there is less time for streaking to occur. Sodium carbonate may be substituted for the borax or the amount of borax may be increased to make a stronger solution.

Be certain to mix all chemicals in the order given and obey any cautionary procedures when using any chemistry. Some suppliers for premixed formulas do exist and may be located through a local photographic store.

PROCEDURE FOR WATER-BATH DEVELOPMENT

While the water-bath process does not work well with modern films, if you wish to experiment with disproportionate development here are some recommendations.

MW-P 20   *Chapter 5, page 56*

For films, a basic water-bath plan appears as follows:

Developer—30 seconds (constant agitation in developer)

Water—1 minute (no agitation in water)

Developer—30 seconds

Water—1 minute

Developer—30 seconds

Water—1 minute

Developer—30 seconds

Water—1 minute

When placed in water, the developer absorbed by the emulsion continues to work for only a short time on the high values before it is exhausted. The lows develop for the time in the developer *and* almost the entire time in the water.

In the example, the high value development probably does not exceed 3 ½ minutes while the lows receive about 6 minutes developing time. It is difficult to be precise concerning actual development times due to the erratic nature of this process.

The water-bath process requires that the film be agitated constantly in the developer. Standard film hangers may result in uneven development and are not recommended. Some plastic film hangers designed for color processing work well.

Today's thin emulsion films do not respond well to the water-bath process. The emulsion cannot carry over enough developer to the water to make it effective. Kodak Super XX Pan, a thick emulsion film, is recommended because it absorbs more developer.

The use of staining developers such as pyrogallic acid (pyro) is not recommended. Staining can be caused by oxidation and the film is repeatedly exposed to air during the transfer from developer to water. Seriously stained negatives have unpredictable printing characteristics and the stain may be uneven. As with most extreme methods some exposure compensation is necessary to maintain the low zones.

I have used the water-bath process with some success on printing papers. If a lower contrast grade is not available or a negative requires an in-between grade, the print can be developed for 30 seconds and transferred to a tray of water for 1 minute. On prints the development of the *low values* is restricted while the *high values* continue to develop. Transfer as many times as necessary but beware of prolonged safelight exposure that may cause fogging. With some papers the contrast reduction can equal ½ paper grade without sacrificing the maximum paper black.

Although a low contrast paper developer will also reduce contrast the water-bath process has the advantage of not having to use a different developer in case other prints require a full strength formula.

PROCEDURE FOR USING DILUTE KODAK HC–110 DEVELOPER

MW-P 21 *Chapter 5,*
page 57

For normal minus two and three developments I use Kodak HC–110 developer that is diluted 1+30 (1 part developer plus 30 parts water) from the *stock solution*. From the commercial bottle (the one in the photo store) the dilution is approximately 1+120. The film is agitated continuously for the first 30 seconds of development and then at 1 minute intervals for 10 seconds each interval. Development times for Tri-X sheet film at 68 degrees F are:

Normal—25 minutes

Normal minus 1—18 minutes

Normal minus 2—15 minutes

Normal minus 3—12 minutes

There is a possibility of slight brownish staining due to the oxidation of the very dilute developer as it works. Densitometers do not measure stain unless they are specially filtered and the negatives may have more contrast than the eye or the densitometer may indicate. Agitation intervals of more than two minutes often cause uneven development. For minus two and three developments an exposure increase of at least one full f-stop is recommended. Personal tests are needed for greater accuracy.

PROCEDURE FOR USE OF HIGH CONTRAST FILMS
Kodak Technical Pan Film (Sheet and Roll Film)

MW-P 22 *Chapter 5,*
page 59

In HC–110 developer I use an exposure index of 25. The exposure index means the *working* film speed for these specific conditions, not necessarily the speed recommended by the manufacturer. This is sufficiently accurate for expansions from N+2 to N+4. I do not recommend HC films for less than an N+2 increase since they are more difficult to handle and most normal films will expand to an N+1 contrast.

I make two exposures. First I find the object I wish to record as my highest textured tone (near white) and place it on zone V. Then I make an exposure giving a zone VI placement. The amount of contrast increase is decided and both negatives are developed together. The two exposures are necessary when severe expansions are planned because the negative density can vary immensely even with small exposure changes. Since they are developed at the same time, their contrast range is the same and the most usable negative can be selected.

I have found that with an N+2 development I usually work with the zone VI placement, with N+4 I find the zone V exposure more workable. The N+3 negatives can go either way, because the exposures are critical.

I develop the film in HC–110 developer 1+15 from stock at 68 degrees F. From the commercial bottle, dilute 1+63.

Times: N + 2   *7 minutes*

N + 3   *9 minutes*   Personal tests are recommended.

N + 4   *11 minutes*

All times are approximate for *tray* development of sheet film with continuous agitation. For roll film agitate at 30 second intervals for 5 seconds each interval. These times are for film that has been pre-soaked in water for at least 30 seconds.

Graphic Arts Films

Graphic arts films vary but can be tested for speed and developed under red safelight by inspection. They have limited field use but are helpful for very low contrast subjects under controlled studio conditions. Their lack of red sensitivity produces unusual gray tone relationships.

CHAPTER 8, SECTION 1 Zone System
Visual Testing Methods

A NOTE ABOUT TESTING

Most photographers begin testing with only vague ideas about what they are really looking for. The resulting landslide of data confuses them and leads to a frustration with photography in general. The manufacturer's recommendations are the easiest solution to the problem but the technical data may be based on priorities that are different than the Zone System's. (See Chapter 6.) If personal data conflicts with the published data it does not necessarily mean either party is wrong. Most probably it is a case of differing standards and interpretations.

Many exposure and development systems have no specific goals. Terminology such as "good detail" or "optimum" development is deliberately vague. One of the reasons testing is important to the Zone System is that a definite visual goal does exist. The specific results can be compared to a known standard.

Fine-tuning a personal system should be approached slowly. The tendency is to throw accuracy and technology at every problem. We try to become more precise in the hopes we can solve artistic problems through greater control. If this were true, any competent technician could produce great photographs.

Personal style stems from the photographer's unique ability to blend technique with personal vision. Precise testing does not insure good photographs, but this is a common misconception of the student when testing is started. Testing facilitates the craft of photography by providing information and experience in handling the materials. Time spent testing will prove to be well invested. The consistency of your photographic technique will be improved and the foundation of applied sensitometry can be used to any degree that suits your personal needs.

The results of highly controlled conditions during testing are almost impossible to obtain in normal working situations. Tests are intended as reference points only but are indispensable if problems are to be solved with a minimum of effort. The simple mechanics of camera operation combined with human error make perfect exposures and ideal contrast ranges the exception and not the rule. Your personal care and criteria will determine how close you come to the mythical "perfect negative."

All of the visual tests can be done in one day if properly organized. Different students can test different films or several tests can be run simultaneously on one film, but care must be taken to insure consistent test methods. A free exchange of information helps everyone and provides a good method of checking results.

TIPS FOR CONSISTENCY IN TESTING

1. An accurate thermometer is essential or the test results have no reference to manufacturers' data or to other photographers' personal tests. In school situations use the same thermometer for all tests if possible and crosscheck several for an average if accuracy is doubted. The best solution is to buy a high quality photographic thermometer for personal tests. I recommend using the 68 degrees F (20° C) standard for all tests.

2. Change only the development time to alter contrast unless you understand the relationships of all other factors involved. In all cases change only one factor at a time or the results may be inconsistent.

3. Test only one film and developer combination at a time and do not switch printing papers. Avoid exotic combinations until you understand testing procedures and can interpret the results accurately. This includes printing papers and developers.

4. Use the same enlarger for all tests. Different light sources will give different results. Always view prints under the same illumination; a combination of daylight and tungsten is good. Do not try to judge prints in direct sunlight. Florescent light will sometimes give dramatically different visual results than tungsten or daylight and should usually be avoided.

   Most printing papers appear slightly darker when dried. The effect of this "dry down" is most noticeable in the high values. Some tones that look pure white when wet, may dry showing slight tone. Judge all test prints when dry.

5. Densitometers may need calibration. Do not assume accuracy and adjust if necessary. Density strips can be purchased from Eastman Kodak Company for calibration.

6. If several people are testing the same film and developer combination, try to standardize test procedures. The data can be compared and several different tests can be run concurrently to save time.

7. *Keep accurate records or the data may be lost or useless.*

8. Some tests require roll film to be cut into strips (normal development test). This should be done *before* development. It is difficult to cut film from reels in the dark, and each strip must be put into a tray or deep tank for stop bath and fixation. The problems with this procedure are obvious. Several reels, each with a separate film strip, can be loaded into deep tanks and removed as needed to complete the processing. Working with a partner is an asset, especially for timing these processes.

9. Use the same zone pair for all tests. This is not essential but helps consistency. (See page 00.)

10. Share your information but be ready to verify any you receive by personal testing.

ZONE PAIRS

The basic structure of Zone System thinking limits itself to the precise placement of one brightness on an exposure zone and the positioning of one brightness on another zone by development.

We *place* one low zone and develop to *position* one high zone. Other subjects "fall where they fall" according to their brightness in the scene. With normal development the results are accurate and predictable, but as we depart from the norm we depart from the very precise results in odd ways.

All zones move with development changes, but since they move at different rates the correct exposure and development combination (and any compensation for low zone movement) for two specific zones may not be *technically* correct for two other zones. For instance, the development increase that moves a zone VII to a zone VIII is different than that needed to move a zone VI to a zone VII. Most students choose to work with the full detailed zones of zone III and VII for their tests. They make exposure corrections to adjust the zone III value and use development to locate the zone VII value accurately.

This limitation is not usually a problem in practical work. It is usually ignored in Zone System literature and in most practical Zone System use, but as a matter of accuracy and real control, the zone pair that is used for testing produces precise results only for that pair. It is impractical to test for every possible zone pairing and development combinations but for absolute accuracy there is no Zone System alternative. Other systems have been devised to overcome these problems but they also have their own built-in limits and difficulties. There are no panaceas for photographic tone control.

I recommend the student use the same zone pair for all tests. Any fine-tuning can be inferred or tested for as the need arises.

VISUAL TESTING

It has been suggested that trial and error testing and visual judging takes into account personal tastes and tailors the negative to specific equipment and methods. This is true as far as it goes. The implication is that visual testing is somehow easier and more personally accurate than sensitometric methods. This is not true.

Visual tests are a two-edged sword. They are less accurate in a technical sense and are easily misinterpreted, but they do place a high priority on the final emotional result.

The tests in this section promote the production of custom made negatives. If this fine-tuning is done by purely visual means it *will work* but the built-in tolerance of the Zone System may produce less than optimum results. It compares to building a house by estimation rather than measuring. Either way the house can be built but accurate measuring makes communication and problem solving much easier and saves time.

The visual testing is necessary for those photographers who don't have access to a densitometer or don't know how to use one. They produce a functional control of the photographic process very quickly. Zone System ideas can be used almost immediately and the results are usually more precise than students are accustomed to. Usually, once the visual tests are completed, the same negatives can be used for the sensitometric measurements.

Most "fine-tuning" is not a matter of making new negatives, it is learning how to interpret existing information in more accurate ways.

I recommend the visual tests be done first if the student is not familiar with testing procedures and concepts.

CALIBRATING THE LIGHT METER

Any testing begins with the accurate measurement of light. If all light meters were built to the same standards the need for re-calibration would be reduced. Different priorities in light meter design require us to determine how our meters relate to the Zone System standards.

It doesn't matter what zone our meter places a subject on as long as it always places subject values on the same zone. We calibrate to a known standard to avoid confusion and establish consistency.

The easiest way to calibrate our meters is to compare them to a meter that has already been tested. If we know a light meter consistently places a subject on zone V, we can compare exposure recommendations to determine where our meter is placing values. Even if our meter does not place values precisely on zone V we can use the information to place zones accurately as long as the meter is consistent.

The alternative to a known meter comparison is to measure a known light source. Colleges, photo processing labs, camera repair shops and even a few camera stores are possible sources for reference light sources and a simple formula can be used to determine zone placement.

The square root of the film speed is used as a reference f-stop. The light source intensity, measured in candles per square foot, will determine the proper shutter speed for a zone V exposure.

This is much simpler than it sounds. Since the square root of 64 is 8, if the rated film speed is ISO 64 the reference f-stop is f-8. (See Table T-1 for a list of square roots.) A light source of 125 candles per square foot will measure 1/125 second at f-8 for a zone V exposure (ISO 64 film). If the meter reads 1/60 second at f-8 the meter is overexposing one f-stop. It is placing values on zone VI. If the light source is known to be 250 candles per square foot, the zone V exposure should read 1/250 second at f-8 for ISO 64 film.

For a film speed of ISO 125 the closest reference f-stop is f-11 (ISO 121). If the reference f-stop is 11 and the light source is 125 candles per square foot, the zone V exposure is 1/125 second at f-11.

Light meters may place values on ½ or ¼ zones and can vary in placement as much as 1½ f-stops from zone V. These dramatic deviations occur most often with in-camera metering *systems* that may favor slight overexposure to insure proper placement of skin tones or the preservation of shadow detail in scenic photographs.

Deviations from zone V placement can either be adjusted by a repair technician, by changing the film speed setting, or by adjusting the camera controls to compensate for the deviation.

Select the f-stop that most closely corresponds to the square root of the film speed you are using.

TABLE T-1

	Square Root Table for Film Speeds												
Film Speed	12	25	32	50	64	100	125	160	200	250	320	400	600	800
Square root (approximate) (also approximate f-stop)	3.5	5	5.6	7	8	10	11	13	14	16	18	20	24	29

ZONE SYSTEM TESTING

This chapter has two parts. Section 1 shows methods for visually judging results. They include methods for determining film speed and development times for Zone System use. The student without access to a densitometer should use this section. If finer control is needed the student may continue to the sensitometry section for a description of using the densitometer for testing.

If a densitometer is available I strongly encourage its use. Enormous amounts of time and energy can be saved by applying even a very fundamental use of basic sensitometry. *It will take less time to learn to use the densitometer than to do the trial and error testing.*

Section 2 is an introduction to basic sensitometry and uses it in its most simplistic form. The only mathematics involved are simple addition and subtraction. Since ultimately all results are visually assessed there is no creative disadvantage to the more technical approach.

Some of the negatives and prints from the chapter end tests may be used for the tests in this section, and I urge the reader to read each test description and procedures before doing the actual testing.

Safelight Testing

Before visual test prints are judged, it is important to insure that the safelight is not fogging the printing paper. Fogging gives false results when judging very high values as in the development tests.

To test a safelight, the printing paper should be exposed to produce a light gray tone such as zone VII or VII ½. An opaque object is then placed on the paper and it is exposed to the safelight for approximately 4 to 5 minutes. The paper is then developed normally. If there is a noticeable difference in tone between the covered and the uncovered area, some fogging has occurred.

The initial exposure simulates the exposure that the paper receives when it is exposed to the negative. Both exposures must be made to insure a proper test, as the safelight exposure alone may not be sufficient to produce fog.

TEST #1

Visual Test for Manufacturer's Film Speed and Development Time

This test takes about 20 minutes not counting darkroom time or the time spent assessing prints.

Before we attempt to define the Zone System gray scale, a working gray scale based on the manufacturer's film speed and development time will be determined. We will make a "zone ruler" representing each of the ten zones using the published film data. A zone ruler is one exposure of each zone value that we can use as a reference to compare the results of the manufacturer's standards to the results of Zone System testing standards.

If you do not wish to see the gray scale produced by the manufacturer's data, skip to Test # 2 to begin Zone System tests.

Equipment Needed:

You will need your camera, film, a tripod, a notebook or pad for recording data, and a light meter of known zone placement. As a test target you need a large, single-toned subject, evenly lit, with some degree of texture. A stucco wall in shade or a large piece of coarse fabric hung in open shade are good subjects. If the subject is too light or placed in bright sun it may be difficult to reduce the exposure enough to make the very low zone exposures. *The ability to see texture is important for this test.*

Possible Problems:

f-stops are often more accurate than shutter speeds and they should be used to vary the exposure whenever possible. Use the shutter speeds only if necessary. If the test is made using natural light the results may differ slightly from tests made with tungsten light.

Step-by-Step Procedure:

Step 1. Mount camera on tripod and position so test target fills frame or at least most of the frame. If any other objects are in the frame, be certain they do not affect the light meter readings or cause flare. Try to avoid any bellows extension factors from being too close to the subject, or compensate carefully for them if this is unavoidable. (See Appendix for compensation formula.)

Step 2. Check target for even illumination. If a spot meter is used, scan the target for an average reading. Even small variations are visible in a print and this makes judging more difficult.

Step 3. Focus camera on target. We require a focused image to assess the amount of detail present in each zone.

Step 4. Set light meter for manufacturer's film speed. Meter the test target and make the first exposure by selecting an f-stop/shutter speed combination that places the target on zone I. If your meter reads a zone V value, give four f-stops *less* exposure than the meter indicates. Record the frame number and the exposure data.

Step 5. On the next frame or sheet of film make an exposure that places the target on zone II. This means give one full f-stop *more* exposure than frame or sheet #1. Record the data.

Step 6. Continue to make a series of exposures by increasing the amount of light by one full f-stop for each frame until at least nine exposures are made. You want exposures representing each zone value from one I to zone IX. If you wish to include any other zones then do so, but be certain to record them accurately. Frame or sheet #5 will represent a zone V exposure at the manufacturer's film speed.

Step 7. Process the film according to the manufacturer's specifications.

Step 8. On the grade #2 paper of your choice, print the frame exposed on zone V to match the tone of a 18% gray card in the back of the text. Print all the other frames at the same printing exposure as the zone V print and develop all the prints at the same time. This is essentially a proof sheet with the zone V exposure printed to match the gray card. Include a small portion of the unexposed film edge as a reference black tone. Develop all prints for the recommended normal time to avoid inaccuracy.

Judging the Prints:

These prints represent the gray scale of the film/developer/paper combination that is produced by your personal methods. Since it is in full f-stop increments any in-between tones must be inferred. If the amount of tone and texture does not match the Zone System scale do not be surprised; the standards may differ. (See Chapter 6.)

With even a very quick look at the prints we can determine the progression of tones and the limit of the detailed range. If the relationship of tones produces the quality of prints you desire then you now have an effective film speed and normal development time.

Examine the zone V print value carefully to be sure it closely matches the 18% gray card, then examine the print that corresponds to the zone III exposure. This value should show good detail but will be quite dark. The zone II exposure should also show very slight detail, and the zone I value should have no detail but may show a slight tone above pure black. Between these three values a reasonable crosscheck can be made of the effective film speed. The clear film edge represents a zone 0 value.

If the zone III detail is barely visible and zone II shows no detail, the film speed used is *too high* to produce the Zone System gray scale relationship. More exposure is needed to retain minimal detail in the zone II value and to increase detail in zone III value. The film is *underexposed* for the Zone System gray scale.

If zone II shows good detail and even zone I has some slight detail then the film speed was *too low* and less exposure is needed. The film is *overexposed.*

For finer tuning the test can be run again at ½ f-stop increments or the film speed can be estimated by carefully assessing the gray scale for the proper relationships. While this test does give the working scale for the published film speed with acceptable accuracy, any visual adjustments from this test data are only an approximation of the effective film speed.

Judging for Normal Development:

Printing the zone V exposure to match a gray card also gives us a check on the development of the film. The Zone System norm records five zones with good detail (zones III to VII), and two zones with slight detail (zones II and VIII). The detailed range of the film with the published development can be assessed by an examination of the prints. If the total detailed range (this includes the minimal tone of zones II and VIII), is more than the seven f-stop norm, the development time is less than normal. If fewer than seven zones show detail the development time is more than normal.

Even if the "wrong" zones show detail we can still count the total number of detailed zones for the development estimate. Changing the exposure will shift only the literal zones and not the relationship between them.

For this first approximation it does not matter that the film speed may not be accurate for the Zone System. This test provides a general set of guidelines that can direct us to a more appropriate film speed and development time. It is not intended to take the place of the tests that follow in this section.

More important is that this test gives us a basis for comparison of the Zone System and the manufacturer's standards. It also gives an instant, accurate set of limits that apply to our personal techniques. We know the working gray scale and the textured range of our materials as we are currently using them.

TEST #2
Maximum Black Printing Test

There are as many methods of visual testing as there are photographers. Each has its own advantages and disadvantages but, surprisingly, each can yield good results when carefully done. This test has been designed to allow reasonable accuracy for those students with a minimum of experience in looking at photographs. Many students have difficulty judging what constitutes a zone III value or precisely what "good detail" really is. This test relies on matching a standard gray tone and reduces the need for photographic experience.

Determining film speed by visually examining the extreme low zones has one major advantage over using a zone V value, the lows move very little with development changes so mistakes during development are not as problematic. This is the method used by sensitometrists. They determine film speed by measuring the zone I value and matching a specific density.

When students try to judge a zone III value as having "good detail" there is enough leeway in the term "good" to allow substantial errors. For this reason I have chosen to use zone V as a reference. This is the equivalent of the 18% gray card. It is a known value and it is also in a print value range to which the human eye is very sensitive. Minute changes in tone can be seen in the zone V value and fine-tuning can be done later by assessing the amount of detail in the low zones. Using this procedure also guarantees that when a zone V exposure is printed as an 18% gray tone we can always produce a maximum black from the film edge. If any errors occur they probably will be on the side of overexposure.

It is true a zone V value will move if development is changed and basing the film speed on values that move is an approximation. This movement is not extreme however, and is offset by the ease and accuracy of matching to a standard value.

Purpose of Test:

For any printing paper there is a minimum time that will print the clear (unexposed) edge of the film as pure black. If we expose the print for a longer time than it takes to make zone 0 pure black, we move the other zones down the scale (darker) but the zone 0 can not get any blacker.

If less than this minimum exposure is given to the paper we will not have any pure black. If zone 0 does not print pure black no other value can be black because they are all lighter than zone 0.

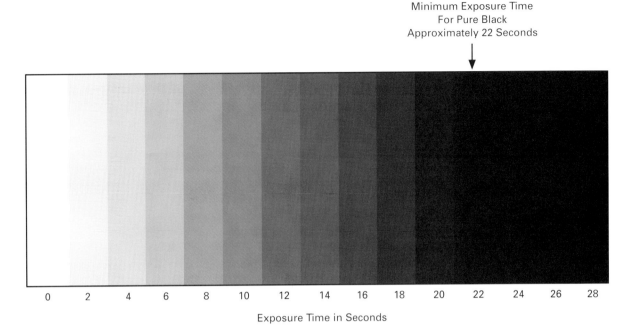

Minimum Exposure Time
For Pure Black
Approximately 22 Seconds

0   2   4   6   8   10 12 14 16 18 20 22 24 26 28

Exposure Time in Seconds

Figure 8.1   *An example of the minimum time, maximum black test strip. In this example the correct minimum time would be approximately 22 seconds. Extreme exposure times may produce slightly deeper blacks, but the first step at which significant change stops is the correct time. The times given are examples only.*

In this test we base the working film speed on the negative that prints as a zone V tone when the zone 0 is printed for the *least* amount of time that will make it pure black on the paper. We will establish the space between zone 0 and zone V so that the proper film speed for zone V will also allow zone 0 to print as pure black. The test takes about 30 to 45 minutes in the darkroom.

Step-by-Step Procedure:

Step 1. Place an unexposed but *developed* negative in the enlarger. In school darkrooms always use the same enlarger to print *all* visual test negatives. Adjust the enlarger height and focus to approximate an 8 × 10 print size. It may be necessary to use another negative to set the focus. The type of enlarger light that you use affects this test. Refer to the appendix for more information concerning enlargers. This test can be done by contact printing if the negative size is large enough to judge.

Step 2. Make a series of exposures on a grade # 2 paper in two or three second intervals. We want a test strip that somewhere along its length produces a pure black. (See Figure 8.1.)

Adjust the printing exposure so that pure black is made between about 15 to 30 seconds. This printing time can be accurately repeated even if a clock is used to time the exposures and it is not so long the paper will suffer from reciprocity departure problems which can affect the data. Extremely short exposures are difficult to control.

Step 3. Process the print normally but do not exceed a two-minute developing time unless the developer specifically requires it. Excessive development will give a false result. *Do not judge the print while wet,* prints appear darker when dry.

Step 4. Examine the dried print and locate the *first step* at which you can no longer detect a change in tone. We want the *minimum* time that produces an effective black. *Do not expose a piece of printing paper to raw light and attempt to match this black.* The negative scatters light and does not produce a black of this intensity unless extremely long exposure times are used. Matching this black would produce an extremely low film speed result.

The longest exposure time on the test strip may be distinctly darker than the first point where the significant change stops. This is the exposure that overcomes the light scattering effect of the negative and produces false results.

Step 5. Repeat the test but use smaller increments of exposure, two-second increments are precise enough. Concentrate on the printing time near the estimated minimum time for maximum black. If the first test shows an approximate time of 25 seconds then concentrate the exposure range for the second test strip in the 20 to 30 second range to be certain of enough exposure latitude. The smaller the exposure increment, the more accurate the test.

Step 6. Re-examine the scale and locate as precisely as possible the *minimum time* for producing maximum black. Record the printing time, the enlarger height, the lens type and focal length, and f-stop used, the paper type, and the print development time and developer temperature.

This test gives us a standard printing time for the *test negatives* in this section. Creative work may not print properly when this time is used. It is a reference standard and does not allow for the flexibility needed for creative photography.

TEST #3
Visual Test for Determining Effective Film Speed
This test takes about 20 minutes excluding darkroom time and time spent judging prints. The target from test # 1 may be used.

Purpose of Test:

Determining a working film speed for a specific film and developer combination. The working speed is also called the exposure index or EI. The ISO speed is based on sensitometric standards. The EI is the speed you are setting on the light meter for your personal use of the film. They are not always the same speed.

Equipment Needed:

Your camera, film, tripod, and a test target. This target can be a large medium-toned mat board (it does not have to be medium gray but it is preferable) or an evenly lit, single-toned subject such as a wall in open shade. You also need a note pad for recording data and a light meter of *known* zone placement.

Possible Problems:

If shutter speeds are used to adjust exposure it may be inaccurate. Using the f-stops is usually more reliable. If the test is done in natural light the results will differ slightly from tests using tungsten lights. It is essential to have accurate shutter speeds to insure correct test results.

Step-by-Step Procedure:

Step 1. Set up or locate test target in even light such as open shade. Check for stray light and reflections.

Step 2. Mount camera on tripod and position so test target fills frame. Beware of shadows cast by you or your equipment and be sure to load the film into the camera.

Step 3. Check target for even illumination. If a spot meter is used, scan the entire target. Focus the camera on *infinity*. No detail is needed for this test, we require only density.

Step 4. Set the light meter at ½ the recommended ISO speed. If the listed speed is ISO 400 set the meter at EI 200.

Step 5. Measure the target and set your camera at an exposure setting that places the target on *zone V*. For instance, if your meter places values on zone V ½ you must give precisely ½ f-stop *less* exposure than your meter indicates. Make one exposure and record the data. Include the frame or sheet number, the f-stop, shutter speed, and film speed used.

Step 6. On the next frame or sheet make an exposure giving ⅓ f-stop less light than Step 5. This is equal to changing the film speed setting on your light meter to the next higher number. On some cameras the increments can only be changed in ½ f-stop steps. The smaller the graduations of change the more accurate the test. If you started with ISO 400 film, you have now made a zone V exposure at EI 200 (Step 5) and a zone V exposure at EI 250.

Step 7. Continue to make a series of exposures, decreasing the light by ⅓ f-stop each time, until a zone V exposure has been made at twice the manufacturer's film speed. In ⅓ f-stop increments this would be a total of seven exposures. Write down all data. For ISO 400 film the data would read as follows:

Exposure # 1	zone V @ EI 200	(shutter speed—f-stop)
Exposure # 2	zone V @ EI 250	"
Exposure # 3	zone V @ EI 320	"
Exposure # 4	zone V @ EI 400	"
Exposure # 5	zone V @ EI 500	"
Exposure # 6	zone V @ EI 640	"
Exposure # 7	zone V @ EI 800	"

Step 8. If roll or 35mm film is used, make at least one exposure with the lens cap on. If sheet film is used the sheet need not be exposed but it *must be developed*. This is a reference zone 0 exposure and is called the *film base plus fog density*. Do not *place* the test target on zone 0 because it might give the film some exposure; it must be absolutely unexposed. If film economy is important, the clear edge of the film may be used but it may be more difficult to judge because of its small size.

Step 9. Process the films at the manufacturer's recommended development time. Use your normal methods, but consistency is important. The data applies to these specific processing conditions only.

Step 10. Print all the negatives from this test at the minimum time for maximum black as determined by test # 2. Select the zone V exposure that most closely matches the standard 18% gray card. The film speed that this negative was exposed at is the approximate exposure index, the EI.

A list of the film speed progression will aid you in selecting the film speed represented by your test exposures. Begin with the film speed recommended by the manufacturer. Each adjacent speed equals a ⅓ f-stop change. Each third number equals a doubling of film speed.

ISO 6, 8, 10, 12, 16, 20, 25, 32, 40, 50, 64, 80, 100, 125, 160, 200, 250, 320, 400, 500, 640, 800, 1000, 1250, 1600, 3200, 4000, 5000, 6400, etc.

TEST #4
Visual Test for Normal Development Time

Purpose of Test:

This test requires about 20 minutes, not including darkroom time or print judging time. After the working EI has been determined, it is possible to find the normal development time for this EI. We will adjust the development time so a zone VIII exposure will print as the lightest zone with some tone.

The test involves making a series of exposures of a scene. The brightnesses of the scene are carefully measured and exposures are made that place at least one easily judged area on zone VIII. The exposures are developed for different times and a normal development time is selected by comparing the zone VIII exposures to a pure white value when printed at the minimum time for black.

Zone VIII was selected as the target zone because when we adjust development to show slight tone for zone VIII it guarantees detail in the zone VII value. If you desire to use zone VII as the high value of your zone pair, the development adjustment is small.

Before beginning it is important to stress that accurate notes should be taken. A mistake in writing down a brightness placement or a zone difference will cause calibration errors.

The selection of subject areas can also be important if the maximum information is to be gained from each negative. Since we base the development time on the zone VIII exposures it is the only value that *must* be right, but the other areas of the scene can be used as cross-reference values.

The zone VIII value should be large enough to judge and evenly toned enough to prevent mistakes in overall effect. Architectural subjects like homes or office buildings generally have broad areas of even tones that make judging the results easier.

Try to find a subject area that logically would be printed as a zone VIII value. Placing an area of low brightness on zone VIII will still work for the test but the scene as a whole may be severely overexposed. Identify as many specific zones as possible on the exposure record for maximum information.

Equipment Needed:

Same as for film speed test except for test target.

Step-by-Step Procedure:

Step 1. Select an outdoor scene with at least one large area of relatively high brightness. White paint in sunlight or a medium-bright, clear sky area are usually logical areas for a zone VIII placement.

Step 2. Measure the target area and select an exposure that places the area on zone VIII. Be sure to use the adjusted EI. Note as many subject areas as possible and on which zone they fall compared to the placed area. If your meter places values on zone V, be sure to give three f-stops *more* exposure than the meter indicates.

Step 3. Make at least five identical exposures of the scene. If roll or 35mm film is used, expose the entire roll at the same exposure. The roll films can be cut into as many strips as is convenient for development (see testing "tips").

Step 4. Develop each sheet or strip of film as follows:

Sheet (or strip) # 1	manufacturer's recommended time
Sheet (or strip) # 2	30% less than manufacturer's time
Sheet (or strip) # 3	15% less than manufacturer's time
Sheet (or strip) # 4	15% more than manufacturer's time
Sheet (or strip) # 5	30% more than manufacturer's time

Step 5. Print all the negatives or one frame from each strip at the minimum time to produce maximum black. A small opaque object like a coin can be placed over part of the zone VIII area to provide a tiny pure white reference. The minimum time, maximum black test should be repeated if any conditions in the darkroom change. This is especially important in school situations where consistency is difficult to maintain. The retest will be very quick because you already have an approximate time.

Step 6. Examine the *dry* prints and select the print that most closely represents the zone VIII tone as a slightly textured value just darker than pure white. The zone VIII will not always show detail but it must show tone. The development time for this negative is the correct normal development time.

If no print matches precisely, estimate the proper time from the closest negative.

Determining Plus and Minus Development

Using the negatives from the film speed and normal development tests we may already have much of the information needed to find the plus and minus times for our film/developer combination. Once we have a normal development time the other negatives used in the tests can be examined to find zone movement. For instance, if we were lucky enough to have zone VII value in the scene we photographed for the normal development test, we can compare the zone VII value at different development times to the zone VIII value at the normal time. The manufacturer's development time may be the correct normal time for us. If this is so, then we can check the zone VII value in the negative developed for 15% more than normal. If the zone VII value looks like a zone VIII we have successfully found the N +1 time. We have moved a zone VII exposure to a zone VIII value with development. If the 15% increase shows the zone VII as darker than zone VIII and the 30% increase shows the zone VIII as lighter than zone VIII, the correct N +1 time is between the two. The correct time can be inferred or the test repeated using development increments close to the suspected time. Without a densitometer it is left to educated guesswork or visual matching.

The effect of decreasing development is assessed the same way. The zone VIII value will not be recorded as the very light textured tone if the development is less than normal. If the 15% decrease moves the slightly textured zone VIII value to a fully detailed zone VII, we have the N-1 time. This kind of approximation does not lead to great precision but it is usually accurate enough for practical work.

Because it may be difficult to judge zone movements without zone references, the next test will provide a set of normally developed zone values. If you feel that you do not need these reference zones to judge values, go to test #6.

TEST #5
Making a Zone Ruler for Comparison

Purpose of Test:

To provide a set of normally exposed and developed zone values to be used for comparison when needed.

This test requires about 20 minutes not including darkroom time or print judging time. If you do not have sufficient information from the negatives already made or you wish to verify or extend your development data, this test provides zone movement references. *This is the same test as test #1 but the corrected EI and development time are used.*

Step-by-Step Procedure:

> Using test target and materials as in the manufacturer's gray scale test makes a series of exposures beginning at *zone I*. Increase the exposure by one full f-stop for each frame or sheet until at least one exposure has been made for zones I through IX. Make one exposure with the lens cap on as a zone 0 reference negative. We want a normally processed frame for each of the ten full zones to which we can compare our other test negatives. *Be certain to use the correct EI and the corrected development times as determined by our previous tests.* This film will be developed *normally* and printed at the minimum time for black test exposure time. Use these reference zone values whenever needed.

TEST #6
Plus Development Test

Purpose of Test:

To determine the development time necessary to move a zone value upward on the zone scale to increase contrast. I have selected the zone recommendations because I feel that using these specific zones for this test insures that detail is retained where it is important, even if minor errors are made. Other zones can be selected for movement if the student desires, but I suggest beginners use these zone values. The student may choose to use a different zone pair for practical work and the adjustments will be minor.

Step-by-Step Procedure:

Step   1. With the test target, as in test #5, make a series of at least three exposures of the zone you wish to move. For an N + 1 development time I recommend making the exposures at zone VII and moving the zone VII value to zone VIII. For an N + 2 time I recommend exposing the film on zone VI and moving it to a zone VIII value.

Step   2. Develop the sheets or the cut film strips from step 1 as follows:

Negative #1   20% more than tested normal time

Negative #2   30% more than tested normal time

Negative #3   40% more than tested normal time

Step   3. Print all negatives at the minimum time for black and compare them to the zone you wanted to move *to*. The development time for the closest match is the approximate plus time. Use the zone ruler prints as references because they represent the zone values as they appear with normal development.

Remember these times do not take low zone movement into account. For the plus development times this is not as critical as for the minus times. Severely overdeveloped negatives may require long printing times if exposure compensations are not made for low zone movement. If none of the developing times are a precise match, the proper time can be estimated or the test repeated.

TEST #7
Minus Development Test

Purpose of Test:

To determine the development time necessary to move zone values downward on the zone scale to reduce contrast. The zone values have been selected for the same reasons as for the plus development test.

Step-by-Step Procedure:

Step   1. For minus developments the test procedure is the same as for the plus development test but the development times are *reduced* from the tested norm in the same increments. For an N-1, make the exposures on zone VIII and move it to a zone VII value. For the N-2 development, place the test exposures on zone VIII and move it to a zone VI value.

Step 2. Process the film as follows:

Negative #1   20% less than tested normal time
Negative #2   30% less than normal
Negative #3   40% less than normal

The developing times for minusing can be estimated by comparing these negative values to the normal zone ruler value by printing them at the minimum time for black.

With the minus times, I strongly recommend that a test for low zone movement be made. The low zones are at a minimum level with normal development. Severe reductions in developing times can seriously degrade the recording of low value detail if no exposure compensation is made.

TEST #8

Test for Low Zone Movement (see MW 7)

Step-by-Step Procedure:

Step 1. With target and materials as in manufacturer's gray scale test make a series of exposures placing the test target on *zone III.*

Step 2. Process the film for the development time you wish to check.

Step 3. Print the negatives at the minimum time for black and compare them to the normal zone values at normal development to determine low zone movement. Record data and compensate as necessary.

Exposure increases will affect all of the zones so the high values will increase along with the lows. This does not alter the development time because we have the same zone relationship when exposure is changed.

CHAPTER 8, SECTION 2 An Introduction to Sensitometry—Basic Testing Using the Densitometer

Many of the tests in this section are the same as the visual tests though some of the zone placements are different. Please read these tests carefully to determine if negatives from previous visual tests can be used for densitometric measurement.

DENSITY

The word density describes the light stopping ability of the negative. A high density refers to the dark areas of the negative where the build-up of silver particles is the heaviest. These areas block the most light. A low density allows more of the light to pass through because there is very little silver image to block it. These are the clearer parts of the negative that we can see through most easily.

Each zone value represents a certain amount of density. The higher the zone the higher the density. When densities are measured by a special instrument called a densitometer, a decimal number can be assigned to the zone value—the higher the number, the higher the zone value. For instance, a density number of 2.0 represents a higher density (higher zone value) than a density number of 1.0.

Sometimes the word *opacity* is substituted for the word density but opacity is measured using a different numbering system. Density numbers do not apply to the term opacity even though the words stand for the same thing.

If we graph the densities of a negative using a bar graph, a low bar would represent a lower density than a higher bar. The graphs in Chapter 3 are similar but we used the zone numbering system instead of the density numbering system. A sensitometrist (a scientist who works with sensitized materials) works with the same graphs, but the decimal numbering system would be used.

THE DENSITOMETER

A densitometer is a light meter. One type of densitometer measures the reflectance of photographic prints and is called a reflection densitometer. The type used to measure the densities of negatives is called a transmission densitometer. Both kinds give their readings in decimal numbers. The decimal numbers are used because they are more precise than f-stops, shutter speeds, EVs, or zones. A transmission densitometer, the kind that measures negative densities, gives a higher number for a higher density. A density of .24 is an average reading for a zone II value, and 1.35 is an average zone VIII density. These are increments for measuring film densities and the reasons for the numbers are not important at this point. We can assign density numbers to any zone by measuring them. If we measure enough approximate zone V values, we can determine an average zone V density that will be correct for many film and paper combinations. Specific papers and films will vary but not tremendously.

We can use the numbers to match film densities to specific zones and be extremely precise in our testing. Visual tests can only approximate this accuracy. If we know the density of the zone VII value we can make several exposures on zone VII, develop them for different times and then measure them on the densitometer. We can compare these measurements to the ideal average density for a zone VII negative value. There is no need to perform maximum black printing tests or rely on a complex visual matching method.

This is *basic, applied* sensitometry and the methods are limited in their applications. A trained technician can deduce large amounts of information from a minimum of tests. Exposure and development data can be plotted from the measurements and precise times pinpointed for specific uses. In the normal development portion of this section, a list of average zone densities is given as reference points. These will function well for most film and paper combinations. Specific testing methods for precise combinations are discussed later in this section.

The newcomer to sensitometry needs to know these are numbers that scientists substitute for the zone numbers. They are used for accuracy and consistency, but they are only units of measurement like feet, meters or zones. For Zone System applications on a basic level we only need to be able to measure the density and use it as a precise point of reference. For a complete understanding of the photographic process there is no substitute for sensitometry. Artists and technicians alike can benefit from the understanding of the process and a sensible application of sensitometry as it functions in producing the type of photographs they want.

Be certain to consider any negatives from previous tests for possible measurements before conducting tests in this section.

CHARACTERISTIC CURVES

Characteristic curves are a graphic display of how film responds to exposure and development. Most students can read a simple bar graph, and learning to use curves begins with this type of display.

Figure 8.2 graphs the relative amount of silver used to build film densities at a normal development time. If the bar graph is thought of as representing a piece of film seen edge on, it is easy to imagine the build-up of silver in the emulsion. The greater the exposure or the development the more silver is built-up.

The difference in the height of the bars in the graph shows the difference in zones. They represent the film densities and their light stopping characteristics.

The bar graph works well when defining zones because each zone is represented as a single density, the midpoint density of the zone graduation. If we want to graph the graduation within a zone we must break it

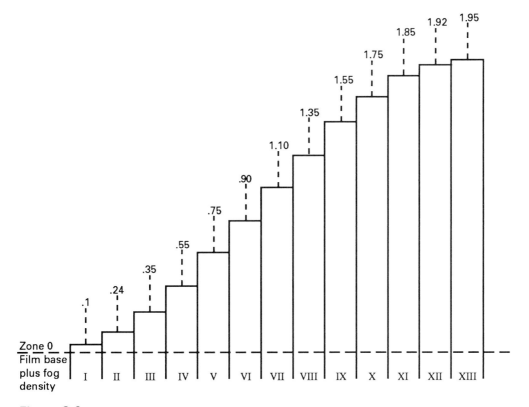

Figure 8.2 *The average midpoint density for each zone is marked on this bar graph. All numbers indicate the measured density above the film base (zone 0) reading. To figure the absolute density, these values must be added to the film base reading. A film base reading is not listed because it varies with the film type.*

down into smaller increments. This can be done by using the decimal numbers. We might use numbers like 1/10 or 1/100 of a zone but this soon defeats the entire concept of the "zone." It is also difficult to decide where one zone ends and another begins. The decimal numbers eliminate this problem entirely but they also eliminate the "zone." (See Figure 8.3.)

A characteristic curve comes from breaking down the bar graph into densities represented by decimal numbers and then drawing a line connecting these finer increments. It is the same as drawing a line across the midpoints of the bars of the graph but the graduations are much smaller. (See Figure 8.4.)

This "line" actually bends because film does not build up densities evenly. When we increase a zone I exposure to a zone II exposure, we do not build up as much of a density difference as between a zone V and a zone VI. This is a normal response of film to light and is a part of photography that must be accepted. Even if the exposure change is the same, different zones build up different densities depending on their position on the scale. Remember, we have defined our own gray scale but it does not mean the zone differences are equal. It just means the normal zone scale is represented by the tones in our scale in Chapter 1.

If we draw a line across two low zone points on the graph and then another across two mid zones, we see that one line is at a steeper angle than the other (Figure 8.5). The steeper the angle of the line the greater

Figure 8.3 *A line drawn across the midpoints of each zone can be used to divide the density values into much smaller increments. The boldface numbers indicate the midpoint densities and the other numbers show measurements made in between full zones. A density can be assigned to any point on the line. When this line connects all of the film densities it becomes the characteristic curve line.*

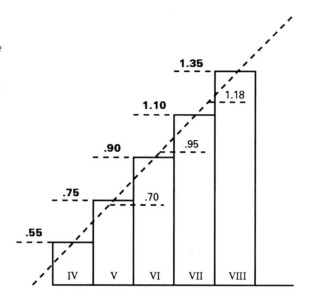

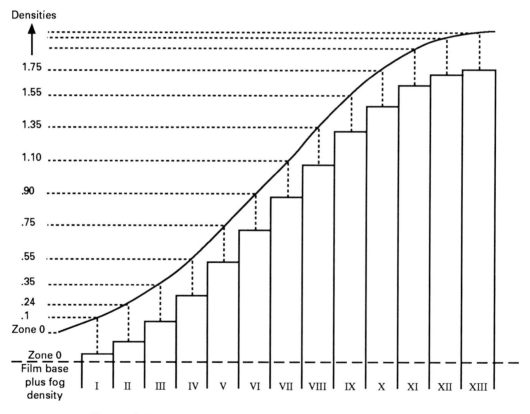

Figure 8.4 *A representative characteristic curve with midpoint densities marked. Note that the spacing of zones is uneven. This shows that the amount of in-between tones (subtle tones between full zones) is not even. Densities above zone X are arbitrary. MW 1 discusses the differences in ''zone size.''*

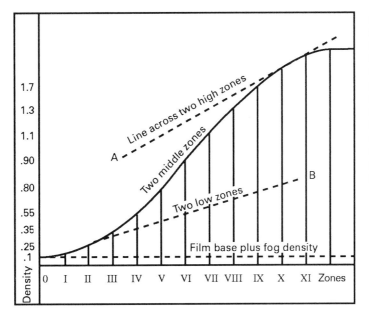

Figure 8.5 *The angle of any section of the characteristic curve can be compared to other sections to show the different contrast responses of a film. Lines drawn across two very high zones (line A) or two very low zones (line B) are not as steep as two zones from the middle of the curve. The steeper the line angle the greater the contrast.*

the contrast. By comparing the angle of the lines we can see that there is less contrast in the extreme low zones and the extreme high zones than those in the middle of the scale.

Using the curves we can compare the contrast of different parts of one film, or how the entire scale of that film responds to development changes. In a more general way we could compare two different films and their responses to exposure and development by looking at the characteristic curves supplied by their manufacturer. This can save us much personal testing time. (See Figure 8.6-A&B.)

The curves are divided into three main sections. The lower curving section is called the toe and usually graphs zones I, II and III. Occasionally, zone IV will fall on the toe of the curve. (See Figure 8.7.)

The straighter part of the curve is called the straight line section and usually represents the rest of the usable zones, zones IV to IX.

If there is an extremely bright value in the scene or we continue to give more exposure, this will be represented on the upper curved section called the shoulder. Zone values as low as zone IX may fall on the shoulder of some films or the value may approach zone XI before falling on the shoulder. When severely overexposed, films will show reduced contrast due to this "shouldering" effect. Each film has a different characteristic curve and this curve varies with the exposure and development.

Zone System workers express the contrast of films in terms of zone movements or relationships, whereas a sensitometrist uses characteristic curves and the mathematical formulas associated with them. The Zone System terms make visualization easier and express emotional relationships well. Sensitometry provides accuracy and a set of mathematical relationships that are universally understood. Each method has advantages.

Curves in this text use zone numbers to indicate exposure changes, but true curves may use logarithmic numbers or lux second references to indicate exposure.

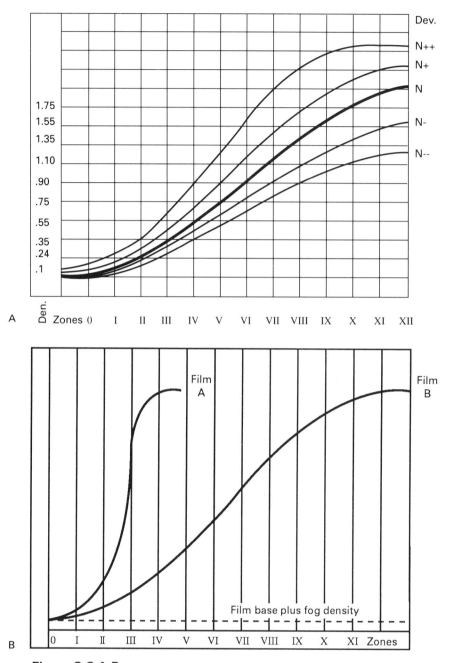

Figure 8.6 A,B *A "family" of curves representing different development times is shown in Figure A. The steepness and the shape of the curve changes with different developments. The movement of individual zones can be traced by comparing density values at different development times. These curves do not represent a specific film.*

The general contrast relationship of two films is compared in Figure B. Even without density values the steepness of the curve of film A shows much greater contrast than film B. When comparing films it is essential that the curves be drawn to the same scale. Some curves use logarithmic exposure numbers, and some curves are plotted using lux seconds (a unit of light measurement) for relative exposure. Zones are usually not used in a manufacturer's curve data but are used in this text to introduce the concept of curve relationships on a simplified level.

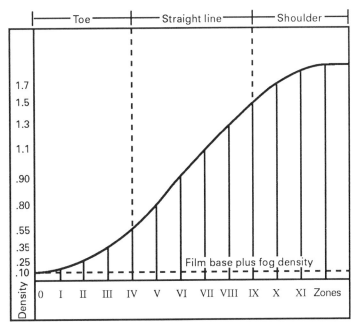

Figure 8.7 *A characteristic curve is divided into three general sections. The "toe" is the lower curving section and usually includes zone 0 through III, and sometimes IV. The middle is called the "straight line" section and includes the rest of the normally used zone values. The upper curving section is called the "shoulder" and begins at different zone values on different films.*

This text cannot cover the intricacies of characteristic curves and how to use them to the greatest advantage. I introduce them to the reader as a way to express and communicate the technique of photography with greater precision, and I recommend that the serious student fully explore their use.

ZONE 0 AS A REFERENCE POINT

In sensitometry all zones have a density number. Since a zone is not a specific point but rather an area of very similar densities, the number reflects an average value for the zone, approximately the midpoint of the densities that could be considered as the zone. For instance, a zone V value density for one film/paper combination could be .72 and for another combination it might be .82, so we strike an average of .75 and call it the zone V density. This is the interpretive leeway that frustrates sensitometrists when they discuss the Zone System. A zone cannot be pinned down as precisely as a sensitometric number. Zone I has been defined as the first tone that can be distinguished from pure black. This does not mean that zone I can always be seen in the print; if the film densities are even slightly off, the zone I value may be lost even though the rest of the zones are within the tolerance of those zones. There is little margin for error when the density is almost black to begin with. Every paper also has a different response to the very low values so that a zone I for one paper might not work for another.

We are again forced to strike an average negative density for a zone I value and it is commonly agreed this density should be .1 *above* the density of the clear, unexposed edge of the film which is the lowest possible density of the film. The clear edge has no exposure so it must be zone 0. This relatively clear edge density is called the *film base plus fog* density because it includes the film's base material and the density of the film's emulsion when it has been developed (the fog), even without any exposure.

The zone I density varies with the film and developer combination because the clear edge density varies from film to film. Every zone I density is measured against the reference point of the zone 0 density.

Some film edges measure .08, some measure .1, and some measure much higher. For each film the proper zone I density is .1 + the edge density. If .08 is the edge (zone 0) density then the zone I density is .08 + .1 = .18. The zone I density for a zone 0 reading of .1 is .1 + .1 = .2.

All of the densities in the chart in the normal development section (page 119) are given in relation to the film base plus fog density. To obtain the *total* negative density, these numbers must be *added* to the film base plus fog density for the film you use.

The film speed test is designed to determine a .1 above the film base plus fog density for a zone I exposure.

NORMAL DEVELOPMENT

The negative is capable of recording more than 10 zones. The density becomes greater as more exposure is given but the detail is not lost. Most modern films record detail as high as zone X and higher. The detail is lost when the negative is printed because the photographic paper cannot record the wide difference in densities as detailed values. A grade #2 paper will record about five zones of density difference with good detail and a total range of about seven zones with very slight tone at each end of the scale. This corresponds with the Zone System scale as we have defined it and is the basis for determining the normal development time. We attempt to make a range of negative densities that will print a seven zone difference as detailed values on what is considered a "normal" contrast paper.

If a brightness difference of seven f-stops in a scene is recorded on the film to print with detail on a grade #2 paper, we have achieved normal development. This does not include the accent zones of 0, I and IX since they are not detailed zones.

A brightness difference of more than seven zones cannot be printed with detail on a normal paper unless the total negative density difference can be made to record like a seven zone difference on the negative. This is what we do when we give a minus development. We decrease the development until a brightness difference of *more* than seven exposure zones is recorded as a density difference of only seven zones. When we give a plus development we are trying to make a brightness difference of less than seven zones look like a seven zone difference in density on the film.

In Zone System terms the mathematics are simple. If we have a paper that will only record seven zones and we have a negative that has eight zones we want to print with detail, we have a problem. We can either use a paper that will record eight zones with detail, or we can make a new negative and record the eight zone scene difference as a seven zone difference in density.

The numbers in sensitometry are used the same way. We measure a low zone density that we want to print and we measure a high zone density we want to print and we subtract the low number from the high. If this number matches the density range number of the paper, we can print both zones on that paper. If the difference in density is lower than the paper number, we can print more zones on that paper. The contrast of the negative is too low. If the density range number is higher than the paper number, both zones cannot be printed on that grade of paper.

TABLE T-2

Zone	List of Zone Densities Density	
0	Film base plus fog	*All densities given are*
I	.10	*above film base plus fog.*
II	.24	
III	.35	
IV	.55	
V	.75	
VI	.90	
VII	1.10	
VIII	1.35	
IX	1.55	
X	1.75	

When the number of zones on the negative is too high for the paper we must reduce it; we minus the development. When the number of zones we want to record is less than the paper can hold, we must give it a plus development or we will get a print with less than normal contrast.

In sensitometry, if the paper density range number is 1.0 and the density difference between zones is 1.3, we must also subtract. When the numbers match, both zones print as the extreme values of the print.

The density numbers that represent various zones are listed in Table T-2. Each film and developer combination produces slightly different numbers and specific papers may require variations of these densities.

These numbers represent a normal set of average negative densities for contact printing or diffusion enlargement on the average grade #2 paper. For condenser enlargement, the development would be decreased to produce slightly lower densities. (See Appendix on enlarger light sources.)

My personal density numbers are slightly higher than these averages, which shows the need for personal testing.

Using these numbers as examples we can subtract the low zone density (zone II) from the high zone density (zone VIII) and get a density range number.

In this case
$$\begin{array}{rl} 1.35 & \text{zone VIII} \\ -.24 & \text{zone II} \\ \hline 1.11 & \text{density range (DR)} \end{array}$$

A paper grade with a DR number of 1.1 would precisely match this negative. If we want to include zone IX as a detailed zone, we subtract the zone II density from the zone IX density to get a DR of 1.31. We need a paper of this DR to print both these zones. This would be a paper of lower than normal contrast.

The total density range of a paper is higher than its detailed range. The detailed zone range usually runs from zone II to zone VIII and does not include zone 0 or 1. The manufacturer's published density range is usually a total range. In Zone System terms we use the zone numbers to express contrast. In sensitometry we use the density numbers to express contrast but the concept is the same. On this basic level all that is needed is to read the film densities on the densitometer and match the numbers.

TEST #1
Determining Effective Film Speed

Purpose:

Determining a working film speed for a specific film and developer combination. The working speed is also called the exposure index, or EI. The ISO speed is based on sensitometric standards. The EI is the speed we are setting on the light meter for our personal use of the film. They are not always the same speed.

Equipment Needed:

A densitometer for measuring the results, your camera, film, tripod, and a test target. This target can be a large medium-toned mat board (it does not have to be gray but it is preferable) or an evenly lit, single-toned subject such as a wall in open shade. You also need a note pad for recording data and a light meter of *known* zone placement.

Possible Problems:

If shutter speeds are used to adjust exposure, inaccuracies can result. Using the f-stops is usually more reliable. With very fast films it may require a darker than average test target or it may be difficult to reduce exposure enough to make the zone I exposure. If the test is done in natural light the results will differ slightly from tests using tungsten light. It is essential to have accurate shutter speed information.

Step-by-Step Procedure:

Step 1. Set up or locate test target in even light such as open shade. Check for stray light and reflections.

Step 2. Mount camera on tripod and position so test target fills frame. Beware of shadows cast by you or your equipment and be sure to load the film into the camera.

Step 3. Check target for even illumination. If a spot meter is used, scan the entire target. Focus the camera on *infinity*. No detail is needed for this test; only density is required.

Step 4. Set the light meter at ½ the recommended ISO speed. If the listed speed is ISO 400, set the meter at EI 200.

Step 5. Measure the target and set your camera at an exposure setting that places the target on *zone I.* For instance, if your meter places values on zone V you must give precisely four f-stops *less* exposure than your meter indicates. Make one exposure and record the data. Include the frame or sheet number, the f-stop, shutter speed, and film speed used.

Step 6. On the next frame or sheet of film make an exposure giving ⅓ f-stop less light than Step 5. This is equal to changing the film speed setting on your light meter to the next higher number. On some cameras the lens openings can only be changed in ½ f-stop steps. The smaller the graduations of change the more accurate the test. If you started with ISO 400 film, you have now made a zone I exposure at EI 200 (Step 5) and a zone I exposure at EI 250.

Step 7. Continue to make a series of exposures, decreasing the light by ⅓ f-stop each time until a zone I exposure has been made at twice the manufacturer's film speed. In ⅓ stop increments this would be a total of seven exposures. Write down all data. For ISO 400 film the data might read as follows:

Exposure #1	zone I @ EI 200	(shutter speed—f-stop)
Exposure #2	zone I @ EI 250	"
Exposure #3	zone I @ EI 320	"
Exposure #4	zone I @ EI 400	"
Exposure #5	zone I @ EI 500	"
Exposure #6	zone I @ EI 640	"
Exposure #7	zone I @ EI 800	"

Step 8. If roll or 35mm film is used, make a final exposure with the lens cap on. If sheet film is used the sheet need not be exposed, but it must be developed. This is the reference zone 0, the *film base plus fog density* exposure. Do not *place* the test target on zone 0 because it might give the film some exposure. It must be absolutely unexposed. If film economy is important the clear edge of the film may be used.

Step 9. This step is optional but can provide much useful information. If you wish to expose the remaining frames of the roll or to use more sheet film for development information, the test can be repeated but with different placement. Repeat the test but make a series of *zone VIII* exposures at the different film speeds. Process these films with the zone I test exposures.

Step 10. Process the film as per the manufacturer's recommended development time. Use your normal methods but remember that consistency is important. The data applies to these specific processing conditions.

Step 11: Using the densitometer, measure the unexposed but developed frame or the clear film edge. Then measure the zone I exposure frames. To the density of the zone 0 exposure add .10. Select the zone I exposure that most closely matches the total of the zone 0 exposure plus the .10 value. This EI is the proper film speed.

For example, if the zone 0 negative measures .09, add .10 to that number to get the proper zone I density: zone 0 = .09, .09 + .10 = .19. The value .19 is the density that the correct zone I value should read on the densitometer. If the zone 0 negative reads .10, zone I should read .1 + .1, or .2.

A list of the film speed progression will aid you in selecting the film speed represented by the manufacturer. Each higher speed equals a ⅓ f-stop increase. Each third number equals a doubling of film speed.

ISO Film Speed Numbers

6, 8, 10, 12, 16, 20, 25, 32, 40, 50, 64, 80, 100, 125, 160, 200, 250, 320, 400, 500, 640, 800, 1000, 1250, 1600, 3200, 4000, 5000, 6400, etc.

If you chose to complete optional Step #9 you will also have a set of zone VIII negatives at various film speeds. The average density value for zone VIII can be found on page 119. The zone VIII exposure that was made at the *same film speed that produced the correct zone I density* can be read on the densitometer and its density can be compared to the average zone VIII density. If the density is too low, the development time must be increased. If the density is too high, the development time must be decreased.

TEST #2
Determining Normal Development

In a sense we are running the sensitometric tests in reverse order. Normal development time is based on how many zones we wish to record with detail and the film speed is based on this development time producing a specific zone I density. In this text the order of the tests is one of convenience and the accuracy of them is far greater than the needs of the average photographer.

Proper sensitometric procedure requires more than just a functional understanding of the process. It is easier for the student to use the average film density for zone I and then adjust the development to that average. The results are so close to the sensitometric standards they could not be adjusted more accurately on the average light meter and camera controls.

After the working film speed (EI) is determined, we can adjust the development time to allow the zone II and the zone VIII values to print as the extremes of the textured range of a grade #2 paper.

The degree of accuracy you require determines the test procedure. If you have standardized on a specific grade and brand of photographic paper, the negative can be precisely matched using the method in test #4. Using test #4 data, the density of the zone VIII value will be more precise than the average zone densities given on page 119.

The procedure in this test will make a negative of the approximate densities required to print a textured range of zone II to zone VIII on the average grade #2 paper.

What is Needed for the Text:

Same as for film speed test.

Possible Problems:

Same as for film speed test.

Step-by-Step Procedure:

Step 1. Set or locate the test target in even light such as open shade. Check for stray light or reflections.

Step 2. Mount camera on tripod and position so test target fills frame. Beware of shadows cast by you or your equipment and be sure the camera is loaded.

Step 3. Check target for even illumination. If a spot meter is used, scan the entire target. Focus the camera on infinity. No detail is needed for this test.

Step 4. Set the light meter at the proper EI *as determined by tests.*

Step 5. Measure the target and select an exposure that will place the target on zone VIII. If your meter places values on zone V you must open up three full f-stops from the indicated setting. Record data.

Step 6. Expose at least five sheets of film at this exposure. If roll or 35 mm film is used, expose the entire roll at precisely the same exposure. The roll films can be cut into strips for development.

Step 7. Develop each sheet or strip of film as follows:

Sheet (or strip) #1   manufacturer's recommended time

Sheet (or strip) #2   30% less than manufacturer's time

Sheet (or strip) #3   20% less than manufacturer's time

Sheet (or strip) #4   20% more than manufacturer's time

Sheet (or strip) #5   30% more than manufacturer's time

Step 8. Measure all negative densities on the densitometer. The development time for the zone VIII density that most closely matches the average zone VIII density is the correct normal development time. If none match precisely, the correct time can be inferred. Development can be adjusted for specific paper-developer combinations by finding the specific density range for the paper (Test # 4). Be certain to take into account the type of enlarging light source that will be used. These negatives will provide important information for the plus and minus development times tests.

TEST #3
Determining Plus and Minus Development Times

The negatives from the normal development time test can be used to approximate the development times for plus and minus developments. Since all the exposures were made at a zone VIII placement we can measure each negative and determine how much the zone VIII value has moved. If any of the negatives from the normal development test are close in density to the average zone VII density, this indicates we have moved a zone VIII exposure down to a zone VII density. This is an N-1 development. We note the development time for this negative and record it as the N-1 time.

If any of the negatives match or come close to matching the density of the zone IX value, we have established a normal plus one development time. This time may be slightly inaccurate for normal photography because it is unusual to move a textured value to an untextured one (zone VIII to zone IX).

If you cannot infer the plus development time, or you require greater precision, conduct Test #3.

For normal plus development:

Equipment Needed:

Same as for normal development test.

Possible Problems:

Same as for normal development test.

Step-by-Step Procedure:

Step 1. Using test target for normal development test make a series of at least four exposures of the target placed on zone VII.

Step 2. Develop films as follows:

Sheet (or strip) #1   20%   more than corrected normal time

Sheet (or strip) #2   30%   ''

Sheet (or strip) #3   40%   ''

Sheet (or strip) #4   50%   ''

Step 3. Measure these negatives and compare them to the average zone densities to determine the amount of zone movement. If the placed zone VII value reaches a zone VIII density, it indicates a plus 1 development time. If it reaches a zone IX density, it indicates a normal plus 2 increase.

For the normal minus developments, *reduce* the development times by the same percentages and match density values to the lower average zone densities. I suggest placing the target on zone VIII and matching zone VII and VI densities.

The more extreme plus or minus times can be conducted in the same manner as this test but the development variations should be extended.

The movement of the low zones must be considered at each development time. *Test #5 is strongly recommended for the plus 2 and minus 2 developments.* Remember the zones you chose to base your data upon are the only zones it is completely accurate for. This is also true for any exposure compensations for low zone movement. In practice, the compensations will work reasonably well for the average photographer and for most zone pairs even if only one pair is tested. The most common zone pair is zone III and zone VII.

TEST #4

Determining a Specific Zone VIII Density for a Paper

Finding the density range for a specific brand of photographic paper and developer combination requires a calibrated step tablet. The Kodak step tablets come in increments of 11 steps or 21 steps. The 21 step tablet is more accurate and I recommend it. These tablets are essentially a set of factory calibrated densities that are used to figure the density difference a paper will reproduce. The step tablet is also available in an uncalibrated model but it cannot be used unless you are willing to measure and mark the densities yourself before the test.

The test will determine the density difference the paper will reproduce. The densities of the negative can then be adjusted to the specific requirements of the paper instead of averaging the results.

Equipment Needed:

A Kodak calibrated step tablet (21 steps), the paper you wish to test, and printing facilities.

Step-by-Step Procedure

Step 1. Contact print the step tablet on the selected paper. Adjust the printing exposure so the first few steps (the clearest steps) of the tablet are recorded as pure black.

Step 2. Process the print at the manufacturer's developing time and *dry before judging.*

Step 3. Examine the print and find the step where the first tone below pure white appears and note the density of the tablet section that produces it. Find the lowest tone before the steps turn completely black. You want the last perceptible gray tone that is not pure black. Note the density of this step.

Step 4. Subtract the low density value from the high density value.

Step 5. The number you get is the total density range of the paper under these processing conditions. Remember, this is the total range and not the textured range.

Step 6. Add the density range number from Step 4 to the zone I density that you determined in the film speed test. This total density is the specific zone VIII density for the paper and developer combination you are using.

Step 7. Conduct the normal development test but match the zone VIII density from this test rather than the average zone VIII density.

TEST #5

Determining Low Zone Movement

I think it is obvious by now that most of the testing in this section is matching densities. To find low zone movement, it is necessary to make a series of exposures of the selected low zone, develop the negatives at the normal minus and normal plus times, and compare their densities with the normal low value densities. Precision beyond ⅓ f-stop increments can be obtained, but if you cannot set the light meter or camera controls with greater precision than + or − ⅓ stop, the advantages are dubious. The consequences of low zone movement with *minus development* are more serious than those associated with plus development. (See MW 7.)

Equipment Needed:

Same as for normal development test.

Possible Problems:

Same as normal development test.

Step-by-Step Procedure:

Step 1. Set or locate test target as in normal development test and follow the same precautions for metering.

Step 2. Using the proper, tested EI, select an exposure that places the target on the low zone that you wish to check. Make at least one exposure or set of exposures for each development time for which you want information.

Step 3. Process the film at the selected development times and measure the negatives on the densitometer. Compare the densities to those obtained for that zone at normal development.

The exposure corrections must be estimated from the data and another test may be necessary to pinpoint the proper density. This is where a knowledge of characteristic curves can be valuable because the data could be plotted and precise corrections could be inferred. The rudimentary use of the densitometer forces some educated guesswork, but the results are accurate enough for all practical photography.

APPENDIX

LIGHT SOURCES FOR ENLARGING

Many enlargers have interchangeable light sources. By changing the light source, the contrast of the print can be altered. The three basic types of sources are diffusion, condenser, and point source. Diffusion enlargement produces the lowest contrast of the three. Diffusion heads use translucent plastic or glass to diffuse the light source as much as possible. A cold light head is a diffusion enlarger that employs a gaseous tube or fluorescent lamp that produces less heat than an incandescent bulb. The diffusion effect is the same with either illumination. Fluorescent lamps may have a significant afterglow which can continue to expose the paper even after the lamp is turned off.

Condenser heads usually use a frosted tungsten bulb and a set of large glass lenses to focus the light. This focusing of light is called columnating, as in straightening the light into columns. When this columnated light strikes the silver image, some of it is scattered into the air and the film emulsion and does not reach the paper. The higher zones scatter the light more than the lower zones and give the paper less exposure than they would using a diffusion light source. This makes the high zones print lighter and increases the contrast of the print. This scattering of light is called the Callier Effect.

A point source head is a type of extreme condenser that uses a pinpoint lamp to gain maximum contrast in the print.

Each type of enlarger head is useful for different effects, and the type of head to be used must be considered when testing begins. Development times are different for negatives when they are printed with different light sources.

When the condenser enlarger is used, the contrast increase is similar to increasing the development time of the negative. The higher zones are affected more than the lower zones. A zone VII value in the negative might print as high as a zone VIII tone while the lower zones remain almost normal. In a practical sense, this means that if we are printing our negatives on condenser enlargers, the normal development time will be less than the time needed for negatives scaled for diffusion enlargement. We need less contrast in the negative to compensate for the scattering of light during enlargement.

Point source enlargers produce the greatest contrast of all. A negative normally scaled for diffusion enlargement would print on a point source enlarger as if it received a substantial plus development. The amount of contrast change can be related in zones but, since each case differs, only in terms of specific equipment and materials.

Tungsten lamps used in condenser enlarging sources do not have the same color output as the cold light sources used for most diffusion enlargements. The exception is the dichroic color heads which usually use a tungsten lamp and sometimes are diffusion heads.

These color differences may create minor contrast differences with graded papers but their effect on variable contrast papers is substantial. It is essential that the color of the light source match the paper's response or published data for contrast filtration may not apply.

Much literature has championed one light source over another and often without any real basis. Each source produces subtly different emotional effects and definite contrast differences. A print made on a diffusion enlarger is extremely difficult to distinguish from a condenser enlargement if the negative contrast is appropriately modified.

There are differences in enlargers but their artistic value can only be judged by the photographer using them. Each has its merits and each is only a tool to be used when it is appropriate.

BELLOWS EXTENSION FACTORS

An f-stop number is derived from the ratio of the size of the lens opening compared to the focal length of the lens. If the diameter of the lens opening is 1/16 of the focal length it represents f/16. It takes sixteen diameters to equal the focal length; f/4 is 1/4 of the local length, etc.

The longer the focal length of the lens, the larger the lens opening must be to maintain the ratio. (See Figure A.1.)

Each lens opening in Figure A.1 represents f/8, but the actual size of the opening is different. Each opening is 1/8 of the focal length. The focal

Figure A.1 *Both lens openings represent an f-8 aperture, though their actual size is different. The marked f-stops are truly accurate only when the lens is focused at infinity.*

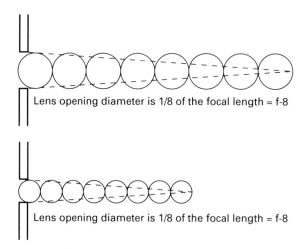

Lens opening diameter is 1/8 of the focal length = f-8

Lens opening diameter is 1/8 of the focal length = f-8

Dotted lines indicate infinity focus (focal length)

lengths of lenses are determined by the distance from the film when focused at infinity, so the f-stop number is only appropriate when the lens is focused at infinity.

When a lens is focused on close objects it is extended beyond the distance that determines the f-number. The opening becomes smaller in relation to the lens to film distance. It becomes effectively a smaller f-stop than what is marked.

Figure A.2 shows that it takes eleven diameters to make up the lens to film distance when focused on a close object. Though marked f–8, this lens opening is acting like an f–11 lens opening. Less light is reaching the film and without adjustment the film will be underexposed.

The amount of compensation needed to correct the exposure for close ups can be determined by the formula $BE^2/FL^2 = $ Exposure factor.

The BE equals the distance from the lens to the film, the bellows extension. FL is the marked focal length of the lens. We square each number by multiplying it by itself and then divide the bellows extension by the focal length. Usually inches are used for measuring the focal length and bellows extension.

If the lens is 8 inches in focal length and the bellows extension is 11 inches we square each number $8 \times 8 = 64$ and $11 \times 11 = 121$ and then divide 121/64 which equals approximately 2. This is a *factor* indicating the needed exposure increase. It means to increase the exposure 2 times, or one full f-stop. If the answer was 4 it indicates a 4 times exposure increase, or two full f-stops. This formula also works in millimeters.

A quick method of figuring compensation is to equate the focal length *in inches* to an f-stop number. An 8-inch lens is f/8, a 4-inch lens is f/4, etc. Measure the bellows extension and equate it to an f-stop also. The difference between the two numbers tells the number of f-stops needed to increase the exposure. To convert: 1 inch equals approximately 25 mm.

If the focal length is 8 inches and the bellows extension is 16 inches, we have a difference of f/8 to f/16, or two f-stops. A two f-stop increase in exposure is needed.

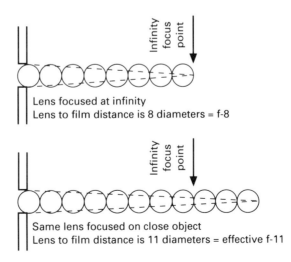

Infinity focus point

Lens focused at infinity
Lens to film distance is 8 diameters = f-8

Infinity focus point

Same lens focused on close object
Lens to film distance is 11 diameters = effective f-11

Dotted lines indicate lens to film distance

Figure A.2   *The effective f-stop is based on its relationship to the lens to film distance that is being used to make the photograph. When the camera is focused on close objects, the lens opening is smaller compared to the actual lens to film distance and less light reaches the film.*

This shortcut works reasonably well and the half stop increments are easy to estimate, but for greatest accuracy use the formula.

A general rule about when to begin figuring bellows extension factors is when you are photographing an object closer than about eight times the focal length. For a 10-inch lens this would be about 80 inches away, or 6 feet. At greater distances the compensation is too small to be needed in normal photography.

The bellows extension factor is needed more often when using large format cameras. The longer focal length lenses require more compensation under the situations commonly photographed, but all cameras are affected in the same way. Very short focal length lenses used on 35mm cameras usually are not affected in practice because the distance to the subject must be extremely close to require compensation.

RECIPROCITY FAILURE

When the light level reaching the film is extremely high or extremely low, the film does not respond to it the same way as when it is within a certain range of intensities. It loses some of its sensitivity to light.

We begin to notice this lack of sensitivity when we require very long (over one second) or very short (under 1/1000 second) exposure times.

If we place a value in a scene and decide that an appropriate exposure is 1/2 second at f/16, we expect the zone value to reproduce as we place it. When the exposure time is increased to two seconds at f/32 the zone value will be underexposed. This failure of the film to respond to an equivalent exposure (f/16 @ 1/2 second = f/32 @ 2 seconds) is called reciprocity departure or failure of the reciprocity law. The reciprocity law states that equal exposures produce equal densities. When the zone value fails to record as we intend it, the law has "failed."

In practical terms, when our exposure times exceed about one second, the light level reaching the film is so low that we must adjust the exposure or it will be underexposed no matter what the meter indicates.

The exposure discrepancy is complicated because the lower the zone the greater the departure from the normal exposure. A zone V value may be underexposed only 1/4 of an f-stop, but a zone II value may be 3/4 of an f-stop underexposed. This effectively increases the contrast of the image. Not only is an exposure compensation needed but the development must also be reduced to compensate for the contrast increase.

Published charts are somewhat vague and are supposed to apply to all black and white films of the same brand, but the Kodak tabular grain films (T-Max) are not as prone to reciprocity failure as conventional films and have their own recommended adjustments. Some conventional films also may react differently.

Unfortunately, since the effect is different at different zone values, the compensations in these charts are, at best, an average. Specific zone value and brightness range information would be more accurate but must be determined by personal testing. (See Figure A.3 A and B.)

Not only is the reciprocity departure more severe as the exposure time increases (lower light levels on the film), but the effectiveness of the compensations are diminished. The lower zones are more affected than the high

Exposure and Development Adjustments
for Long and Short Exposures

If Calculated Exposure Time is (seconds)	Use This Lens-Aperture Adjustment	OR	This Adjusted Exposure Time (seconds)	AND	This Development Adjustment
1/100,000*†‡	+ 1 stop		Adjust aperture		+ 20%
1/10,000*‡	+ 1/2 stop		Adjust aperture		+ 15%
1/1000	None		None		+ 10%§
1/100	None		None		None
1/10	None		None		None
1	+ 1 stop		2		- 10%
10	+ 2 stops		50		- 20%
100	+ 3 stops		1200		- 30%

* Not applicable to EKTAPAN Film.
† Not recommended for TRI-X Pan Professional Film / 4164
‡ Not recommended for ROYAL Pan Film or SUPER-XX Pan Film
§ EKTAPAN Film does not require an adjusted development time at 1/1000 second.

A

Adjustments for Long and Short Exposures
At the exposure times in the table below, compensate for the reciprocity characteristics of these films by increasing the exposure as shown.

If Indicated Exposure Time Is (seconds)	KODAK T-MAX 100 Professional Film			KODAK T-MAX 400 Professional Film		
	Use This Lens-Aperture Adjustment	OR	This Adjusted Exposure Time (seconds)	Use This Lens-Aperture Adjustment	OR	This Adjusted Exposure Time (seconds)
1/10,000	+ 1/3 stop		Change aperature	None		None
1/1000	None		None	None		None
1/100	None		None	None		None
1/10	None		None	None		None
1	+ 1/3 stop		Change aperture	+ 1/3 stop		Change aperture
10	+ 1/2 stop		15	+ 1/2 stop		15
100	+ 1 stop		200	+ 1 1/2 stop		300

B

Figure A.3 A and B "© Eastman Kodak Company. Reprinted courtesy of Eastman Kodak Company."

zones and often show less contrast than normal. When development is decreased to lower the overall contrast the low zones are further affected. Even exposure compensations cannot completely correct this loss of contrast in the lows.

The charts also show the decrease in contrast when extremely short exposure times (high light levels on the film) are used. An increase in development is needed in the rare cases when the exposure time is less than 1/1000 second.

FILTERS

The possibility of errors when visually assessing technical effects is most clearly shown in the use of colored filters for black and white photography. The change in tone relationships is easily misinterpreted. Some modern textbooks persist in stating that a filter can be used to lighten an object of its own color, and visual assessment of the photograph seems to support this theory. When a red object is photographed through a red filter, it is rendered as a lighter tone than when it is photographed without the filter.

The real reason for the lightening of the object is less obvious. It is not possible to get *more* exposure on the film by putting a filter of any kind between the film and the subject. A filter does just what its name implies, it removes or filters something out. A red filter looks red to us because it is removing all of the colors *except* red. Only red light is reaching our eye so the filter looks red. In an idealized situation, when a red object is photographed through a red filter the amount of light reaching the film is almost the same as when no filter is used. All other colors are blocked to various degrees and are recorded much darker than normally. The red object is not lightened; all the other colors are darkened. It is when we add the filter factor that the red object is overexposed and recorded as a very high zone value.

Filter factors are given for all colored filters. The factors indicate the amount of exposure increase that each filter requires. Because the colors found in nature are not pure and neither are the dyes used to manufacture the filters, there is always some loss of light. The factors compensate for these imperfections and are also responsible for the extreme lightening of objects that are the same color as the filter. Using the filter factor *overexposes* any subject that is the same color as the filter.

Figure A.4 illustrates a filter's effect on colors and the overexposure created by the use of the filter factor. Three objects of different colors but equal brightness will record as the same zone on panchromatic film (zone V). When a red filter is used, the red object will record only slightly lower. The other colors will record much lower than normal because most of their light is blocked by the filter. The red object is lightened by the added exposure of the filter factor and records as almost a zone VIII value, while the other objects move upward to low, but detailed, zone values.

The colors of real scenes are mixtures of many different colors, and the actual amount of light reduction is difficult to predict. It is dependent upon the color response of the film, the strength and quality of the filter, the color of the subject, and the color of the illumination. Experience can give a general idea of how much lower objects will record but the variables are numerous.

Filter compensations are given as *factors* and not as f-stop increases. A factor of 2 indicates twice the exposure or one stop. A factor of 8 indicates an 8× increase in exposure or three f-stops. Some manufacturers also list the increase in f-stops.

When using more than one *factor*, they are not added, they are *multiplied*. For instance, if we use a filter with a factor of 2× (one stop) and we calculate a bellows extension factor of 8× (three stops), the total factor is 16× (4 stops). Converting the factors to f-stops and then adding them, or using the exposure record in Chapter 4, will help avoid problems.

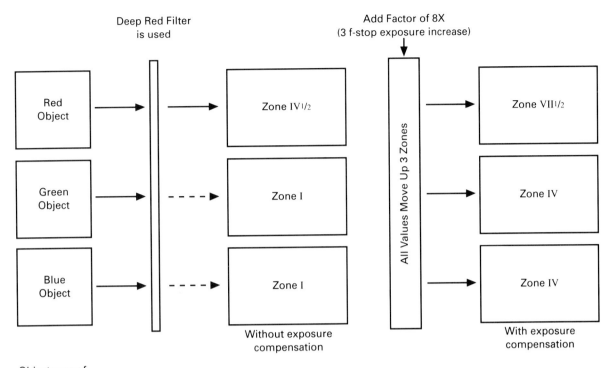

Figure A.4.

Although the red filter has been used as an example, all colored filters work in the same way. A blue filter passes blue light and blocks red and green. A green filter blocks red and blue light. The spectral response differs slightly with each manufacturer.

Neutral tones such as white, gray, and black are minimally affected by filtration except where the colored dyes in the filters act as neutral density. This explains why we can use a strong filter to darken a sky but the clouds are not affected.

AGITATION

The type and frequency of agitation patterns and intervals does not dramatically affect the contrast of the negative. A comparison of the densities with different types of agitation confirms this. The densities show no significant variations in the film response between intermittent and constant agitation patterns. The development *times* that produce these densities are widely varied however.

The inference here is that as long as the interval of agitation is frequent enough to avoid disproportionate development, the only result is to alter the development time.

Constant agitation does not increase the contrast of the negative over intermittent agitation. It decreases the development time needed to attain any specific contrast. The concept of disproportionate development based on selective exhaustion is discussed at length in the description of the water-bath process in Chapter 5.

TABLE A.1

Zones	I	II	III	IV	V	VI	VII	VIII	IX	Agitation
Densities above FBF	.1	.25	.45	.65	.82	1.1	1.25	1.40	1.55	5.5 min. Constant
Densities above FBF	.1	.25	.44	.62	.83	1.05	1.25	1.40	1.53	6.5 min. Intermittent every 1 min.

Table A.1 shows sample film density relationships with different agitation intervals: Data for Kodak Tri-X 4 × 5 sheet film developed in HC-110 dilution B (1 + 7) @ 68 degrees F.

Secondary effects of agitation patterns are more significant. If the pattern is too regular, flow patterns are set up and densities are higher where agitation is consistently greater. This usually occurs near the film edges.

The intensity of agitation affects the development time in the same way as the frequency. The more vigorous the agitation, the less development time is needed. A violent agitation of five seconds duration will decrease the time compared to a gentle agitation of the same duration. The difference is very slight however, because the pattern is still intermittent and the duration of the agitation is very small compared to the development time as a whole. Extremely violent patterns can have serious side effects such as frothing the developer. This causes air bubbles and possibly high edge densities due to faster moving solution near reel spirals or the film hanger edges.

Development times of less than four to five minutes are not recommended for tank development because of the danger of uneven development. Sheet films can be successfully processed in trays for shorter times, but the possibility of problems increases as the time decreases. Changing the developer dilution to obtain a longer working time is a sensible procedure.

The advent of excellent home processing machines has made film development much less burdensome. Though usually designed for color films, they work very well with black and white materials and can be adjusted for constant or intermittent agitation patterns.

Space limitations in this text make a complete discussion of agitation patterns impossible, but some general information can be helpful in saving time for the beginner.

The goal of agitation is to replace exhausted developer with fresh developer. If exhausted developer is not replaced, development will not continue.

To avoid uneven development and insure consistency this replacement must be accomplished following two basic rules:

1. The replacement must be in some pattern or form that is repeatable or you will be unable to duplicate results.
2. The pattern or form of agitation must not set up flow patterns that will cause uneven densities.

The methods that work are numerous, but all of them follow these basic rules (assuming that you want even, consistent development).

I recommend continuous agitation for films developed in trays and intermittent agitation for films developed in hangers or on reels—the difference being that reels and hangers encourage flow patterns around reel edges and through hanger holes. Most students find it easier to set up efficient *intermittent* patterns rather than continuous ones. As long as the agitation interval does not allow disproportionate development, the agitation pattern will only change the development time.

For intermittent agitation I recommend 30-second intervals for most modern films since they tend to have thin emulsion layers and the small amount of absorbed developer exhausts rapidly. Intervals of one minute or more may cause disproportionate development. The greater the dilution of the developer, the shorter the agitation interval must be to avoid disproportionate development.

These recommendations are deliberately generalized because the subject is so complex. Variations in developer formulas, temperature, films, etc. all contribute to the overall effectiveness of agitation, and *any* recommendations are subject to debate. If the method you select accomplishes the goal of agitation and follows the two basic rules, it will work reasonably well. Only experience and *practice* can insure proper method.

SELENIUM TONING OF PRINTS

Diluted selenium toner may be used to alter the color and contrast of printing papers. The toner was originally formulated to produce warm reddish or brownish tones on warm tone papers, but the recent trend has been to use it at high dilutions to produce slightly blue or purple tones on the colder toned papers used in some fine art photography. The toner also gives a slight intensification of the lower print values. The amount of color change and intensification varies with paper type, print developer, and toner dilution so only general recommendations can be made.

Prints to be toned should be carefully examined since there may be some loss of image detail because of the intensification of the blacks.

There are many references to the use of selenium toning to increase the permanence of the print. While the chemical compound formed by toning is known to be more stable than the common silver image, the print permanence is far more affected by the processing methods of the individual. Proper development, fixation, and washing have a more important role in print permanence than selenium toning. Toning is not a guarantee of archival quality and should be considered primarily as a tool of color and intensification.

Procedure for Toning Prints in Selenium

Prints must be developed and fixed completely before toning. If any residual silver compounds are left due to inadequate fixation they will create pinkish stains. Most archival methods recommend a two bath fixing process to insure complete removal of these compounds.

Some photographers use a plain hypo bath (sodium thiosulfate) as a second fixer to reduce the acidity of the print from the first fixing bath. The acidity of the print can affect the evenness of toning. After a brief water rinse the print can be placed directly into the toning bath if the toner is diluted with hypo clearing agent instead of water. If plain water is used to dilute the toner then the print should be neutralized by a brief immersion in a weak solution of sodium sulfite, or Kodak Balanced alkali (Kodalk). A weak (10%) borax solution may also be used.

The toner is diluted 1 + 7 to 1 + 30 depending upon the amount and speed of toning desired. The stronger solutions will generally produce warmer tones than the weaker ones, but this varies with the paper and the difference is usually subtle.

If the toner is mixed with hypo clearing agent the dilution must not be so strong that toning occurs before the hypo clearing agent has time to work. If this happens a second hypo clearing bath is necessary.

My personal method is to treat the prints in a hypo clearing bath *before* toning to neutralize the acid fixer and to insure the print is thoroughly cleared. My toning times are very short even with dilute toner and often would not allow the clearing agent sufficient time to work.

It is difficult to judge the amount of tone while watching the print because the effect is gradual. I use an untoned reference print which I watch with only an occasional glance at the print being toned. Judging prints under fluorescent lighting is very difficult and I recommend either a normal tungsten source or a combination of tungsten and soft daylight, as from a north facing window.

Wash all toning utensils carefully. The toner stains these items and the stain may be transferred to other objects.

REDUCTION AND INTENSIFICATION

Intensification and reduction are terms used to describe post-processing controls of the density and contrast of the negative or print.

While intensification usually implies an increase in density and contrast, some methods of reduction are used to control density with no contrast changes.

The most common techniques for post-processing controls involve changing the relatively stable silver image into a silver compound which can be manipulated easily. The Farmer's reducer formula and the chromium intensifier formula both work in this manner. A second method of intensification uses a concentrated selenium toner to combine with the silver image to create greater density and contrast.

Reduction

This term implies the removal of material from the negative or print. The silver image is literally reduced by chemical means. Farmer's reducer uses potassium ferricyanide and sodium thiosulfate in a kind of two-step process to remove silver. The chemicals are mixed together and the ferricyanide combines with the silver to form a compound. This compound is then removed by the thiosulfate which is the main ingredient of standard fixer.

The reduction of material is not even and the contrast will increase. This is called a cutting reducer because it cuts (removes) low densities more than high densities. In the negative, the shadow areas will be removed first. In the print, the high values are reduced more than the lows. If a negative is severely overexposed, it may exhibit less than normal contrast due to the exposure values falling on the shoulder of the film's characteristic curve.

Disproportionate reducers for changing density and *reducing* contrast by "cutting" the *high* values can be formulated. A good formulary will list several.

Intensification

The two methods of intensification add material to the film or print but do it in slightly different ways. Chromium intensifier first converts the silver to a chromium compound and then the image is developed for a second time to increase density and contrast. An increase in grain is a by-product of this process.

Selenium toning intensification combines the silver and selenium into a stable compound. Since the selenium is darker than silver and combines in proportion to the amount of silver, the high zone densities are increased more than the low zones. The selenium process exhibits little or no grain increase and the contrast can be increased to a plus one contrast level with some films.

Intensification and Reduction Formulas and Procedures for Negatives and Prints

Farmer's Reducer Formula #1
(cutting formula)

Stock Solution A

Potassium Ferricyanide	37.5 grams
Water to make	500.0 ml

Stock Solution B

Sodium Thiosulfate (hypo)	480.0 grams
Water to make	2.0 liters

For use, mix 30 ml solution A with 120 ml solution B and add to one liter of water. Immerse the film or print to be treated in the solution and remove when reduction is sufficient for personal needs. A white tray will assist in judging negative reduction. Wash material thoroughly when reduction is completed, then dry.

This formula is usually used with overexposed negatives when an increase in contrast is needed along with a reduction in density.

A second Farmer's reducer formula may be used when a proportionate decrease in density is needed.

Farmer's Reducer Formula #2
(proportional formula)

Solution A

Potassium Ferricyanide	7.5 grams
Water to make	1.0 liter

Solution B

Sodium Thiosulfate (hypo)	200.0 grams
Water to make	1.0 liter

This method uses the two solutions separately. The film is immersed in solution A for one to three minutes with constant agitation, depending upon the degree of reduction required, and then transferred to solution B for five minutes. The film is then washed thoroughly and dried.

If you are unfamiliar with this process, I recommend the immersion in solution A be kept to a minimum and the process repeated if necessary. This reduces the possibility of over reduction.

The effective life of the *mixed* chemistry is limited so reduction should be done shortly after mixing. All materials to be reduced should be properly fixed and washed. If any doubts exist, it is wise to use an unimportant film or print as a test subject.

On prints, these solutions can be applied locally to reduce small print areas. Avoid contact with the chemistry and apply with cotton swabs or balls. Local reduction of negatives is not recommended without extensive practice or permanent damage may result.

These chemicals can be dangerous if improperly handled. Avoid skin contact and breathing the vapors. Observe all sensible precautions with unknown chemistry.

Chromium Intensifier

This formula is available in packages from Eastman Kodak Company, and I recommend the reader use them. The safe handling of the acid and toxic nature of the generic chemistry requires care and experience.

Chromium Intensifier Formula
Stock Solution

Water	150.00 ml
Potassium Dichromate	90.0 grams
Hydrochloric Acid, C. P.	64.0 ml
Cold water to make	1.0 liter

For use, mix one part stock solution to ten parts water.

The film is immersed in the solution until the image is thoroughly bleached. This action can be visually assessed. The film is then redeveloped in a fast-acting, non-staining developer such as Kodak Dektol for about five minutes in normal room light.

The degree of intensification can be altered by changing the redevelopment time, but the film must be fixed after development if less than maximum intensification is used. The film is then washed and dried.

Developers high in sodium sulfite such as Kodak D-76 and Ilford ID-11 should not be used for redevelopment. The sulfite may dissolve the bleached image before redevelopment can occur.

All materials to be intensified should be properly fixed and washed before attempting this process or staining may occur.

Selenium Toning for Intensification

Although commonly used to alter color and to intensify the blacks in prints, this toner is an excellent intensifier for most films.

The standard toner can be found in many supply houses. For negatives it is mixed 1 + 4 with water. In normal room light the film is immersed for three to five minutes, depending on the degree of intensification required, at 68 degrees F (20 degrees C). It is then washed and dried. The film will show a distinct color change.

Films that have been processed in a staining type developer such as pyrogallic acid may show uneven toning or further staining when toned in selenium. A test film is recommended.

Selenium is a heavy metal compound and must be handled and disposed of properly. Avoid skin contact and breathing the vapors. Observe all sensible precautions.

These particular formulas have been selected as representative of the many that can be used. They are perhaps the safest and most easily formulated, and the chemistry is commonly found in photographic supply stores. Other formulas may be needed for special processes or conditions.

ZONE CALCULATORS

Several zone calculators have been designed as aids for visualization and to increase exposure and development accuracy. The "Zone Systemizer" (see bibliography) designed by Dowdell and Zakia is a generalized zone scale resembling a fan which is part of a calculator dial. The light meter readings are transferred to the systemizer dial and by rotating the dial, exposure and development data can be determined. This includes compensation for low zone movement.

The "Wonder Wheel" developed by Phil Davis is fully described in his text, *Beyond the Zone System*, and detailed plans for its construction are included. This is a systemizer type of device, but it relates to a specific film and paper combination and is divided into much smaller increments for greater precision.

While the "Zone Systemizer" is more directly applicable to the system and is divided into the traditional ten zones, it is only representative of general film response. The "Wonder Wheel" is remarkably accurate for a single film and paper combination but is divided into a 21-step gray scale and does not apply directly to the Zone System.

Both methods require the photographer to carry one more piece of equipment (the calculator), and both add one more opportunity to make an error in transferring the light meter readings from one piece of equipment to another. Both offer the student a visual reference scale that can be easily carried on photo missions and both can increase accuracy if used correctly. They are particularly useful for those students who have difficulty in visualizing gray tones.

THE ZONE SYSTEM AND COLOR FILMS

The general principles of the Zone System can be applied to color photography, but the detailed range of the films is generally shorter and the control of contrast by development changes is very limited. Visualization is also complicated by the emotional effects of colors and the complex variations of color balance that occur when the development is not normal.

A scale of the detailed zones can be determined for any film by conducting the manufacturer's gray scale test (page 96). With color films it is usually necessary to use exposure increments of 1/2 f-stops to insure accuracy. The detailed range often falls in between full zones.

Most transparency films will record detail from zone III 1/2 to zone VII 1/2. There are almost no transition zones and the fall off to maximum black is abrupt below zone III. Pure white is reached quickly beyond zone VII 1/2.

Modern color negative films may show detail as low as zone II 1/2 but this is often lost in printing because the color paper does not record extremely low zones very well. The upper detailed range of the *film* may exceed zone X but this detail cannot be printed with the low values unless masking is used.

Changing the development time from normal will cause a "shifting" of the basic color balance of the film. Increased development of most color films creates an excess of the warmer colors like red and yellow while decreasing development usually shifts the film toward a blue or cyan cast. Because of these color changes the development is not altered if accurate color rendition is necessary. This limits the control of film contrast by development. In most studio and field photography the contrast is more commonly altered by using supplementary lighting or reflectors.

It is possible to compensate for these shifts with correction filters if the development changes are not too severe but the process can be complicated. A color temperature meter and accurate testing are necessary, and the number of compensation filters that may be needed can become costly.

Color films also respond in a slightly different manner to development than black and white films. Commercial photographers often resort to "pushing" (increasing development) and "pulling" (decreasing development) to correct *exposure* errors. The film's response to development is more like changing exposure with many of the zones moving up and down in unison. The contrast of the film is altered but not as much as the overall density. For commercial photography the development changes are used to correct exposure problems and not as a contrast control.

Dowdell and Zakia (The Zone Systemizer) recommend pre-exposure to an 18% gray card to reduce contrast in color films. My personal experience with this method has produced only a slight contrast reduction before a distinct graying of the low values occurs, which I find objectionable. The appearance of the photograph is affected more than sensitometric tests might indicate.

Pre-exposure involves exposing the film to an out-of-focus, single-toned subject like a gray card. The gray card is placed on zone I or II and an overall "fogging" is given to the film. The scene is then exposed on the same piece of film. The pre-exposure affects the low zones by increasing their density. The slight exposure is only a small percentage of the total exposure of the high zones and they are minimally affected. Because the lows are moved upward in density and the highs are virtually the same, the contrast of the film is decreased.

Some black and white developers use a chemical fogging of the film to duplicate the effect of pre-exposure and increase the effective film speed. The density of the lows is increased but this is density with no detail. It is also possible to pre-expose to colored cards which alters the color balance of the low zones as well as the overall contrast.

While pre-exposure does reduce contrast it is difficult to maintain consistency. Color saturation may be decreased and the maximum black of the material may be noticeably affected if the placement of the exposure target is too high.

Some photographers using sheet film will pre-expose several films under controlled conditions and then use these films for field work when needed. See *The Zone System and Flash Photography* for an explanation of how units of exposure are used in pre-exposure techniques.

An effective, though cumbersome method of color contrast control uses different films for different contrast situations. Slide duplicating films have less inherent contrast than the normal pictorial films and can be used to simulate an N− development with excellent results. They are available in both daylight and tungsten balanced forms.

To simulate N+ developments with transparency films, a specialized photomicrography film can be used. These films are used for photography through microscopes and produce higher than normal contrast results. Some corrective filtration may be needed for daylight use. High contrast color negative films are also available from Eastman Kodak and some are daylight balanced.

Reducing contrast with color negative films can be accomplished by a masking technique. A special masking film is exposed in register with the negatives and used to "dodge" the low values during printing. Masks may also be used in printing transparencies and black and white negatives. Recently a light sensitive glass material has been developed as a reusable masking device and offers an alternative to the traditional masking films. Calumet Corporation is one source for this masking glass.

Placing Values on Color Film

Once the detailed zone range is known for a particular film we can adjust the exposure to favor either the high or low zone, depending upon its importance. With transparency films most photographers prefer to maintain high value detail at the expense of the lows unless there is a specific need for low value detail. Viewers generally prefer a slightly darker transparency over a slightly lighter than normal one. The tendency is to place the important high value no higher than zone VII and to let the lows fall where they may. I often place an important high value as low as zone VI 1/2 to insure the greatest color saturation.

Color negative films allow considerable overexposure without serious problems. Many times the low value can be placed as with black and white films and the color film developed normally. This insures low value detail, but it may be necessary to use a masking process to print the high values if the scene contrast is high. Values falling above zone X may not print with detail even with masks.

Because color balancing can be done during printing it is possible to make minor contrast adjustments by changing the development of negative films. I do not recommend more than an N+ 1/2 or N− 1/2 change or the color shift may be severe.

APPLIED TECHNICAL THINKING

Photographer Wynn Bullock had an unusual way of making his famous "foggy" surf photographs. Instead of opening the shutter for an extended time exposure, he would cover the lens until the surf was crashing in precisely the area he wanted and then uncover it for the exposure. He said, "This way, you have control of the character of the 'fog' and its position." He made a series of shorter exposures rather than one long one. This allowed him to manipulate the density of the mist and also gave some control over where the fog appeared. If he didn't want mist to obscure a portion of the photograph, he would expose the film only when that portion was not covered by the moving water.

I relearned this lesson when I attempted a two-minute time exposure of trees in heavy fog (real fog) at Point Lobos. When I developed the film, there was no fog in the scene! The fog had been moving during the exposure. Though I saw the fog, the trees that were generally covered by it appeared long enough to record on the film. It had the effect of seeing right through the fog. I later rephotographed the scene under similar foggy conditions but watched carefully and made incremental exposures when the fog was where I wanted it. I had learned to think of time as a creative tool and not just a technical detail.

I reversed the process when I found it necessary to make a long exposure of a metal sculpture. The extreme viewpoint that represented the sculpture best required a very small f-stop to bring the entire piece into focus. Unfortunately, a vital, aesthetic aspect of the piece was the numerous scintillations of the sun on water that continuously flowed over the metal. A long exposure would show these pinpoint scintillations as streaks of light and destroy the artist's intent.

My solution was to break up the long exposure into a series of very short ones. Instead of one, 1/4 second exposure I made sixteen exposures at 1/60 second. This gave me multiple scintillations (because they moved slightly between exposures), but each one was a point of light, not a streak.

I had not done anything "new" in a technical sense; I had just made an adjustment in how the technique was applied. I made an aesthetic result determine my method.

This thinking has helped me make many photographs that I could not accomplish any other way. I began to look at my equipment and processes as something other than technical aspects. Instead of my tripod being technical equipment that held my camera steady, it became part of the creative process. It slowed me down and forced me to consider every move I made when composing a photograph. My compositions were better because of this mechanical requirement. When I make a compositional change using the tripod, I think about it more carefully.

In my quest for speed and efficiency I discovered that it is not technology that solves my problems but rather my attitude about applying technology. It has helped determine my photographic style and certainly altered the kind of photographs I make.

Accuracy and efficiency only result in accuracy and efficiency. *They do not insure a good photograph; they insure an accurate and efficient photograph.* If we equate these results with "good" photography, then they apply, but if we change the objective of our photographs, we may reduce their importance. If a problem exists there is a tendency among photographers (myself included) to think in terms of another lens or a different developer to solve it, and we are heartily encouraged by the manufacturers of photographic equipment and supplies who have some interest in this approach.

We all hope to find *"THE COMBINATION"* of processes and materials that will give us great photographs, and in certain cases this may be possible. Photography does present situations that only different equipment or materials will make feasible. Unfortunately, some of these problems may be difficult or impossible to solve if technology is the only approach we take. Remember that many great photographs were made without the benefit of the Zone System or a master's understanding of sensitometry. These are information tools and it is how we approach their use that determines their value to our work. Learn them if you desire greater control; they can be invaluable. They cannot and will not make you a good photographer. They can, and do, provide you with the skills you need to make the kind of photographs you want.

THE ZONE SYSTEM AND FLASH PHOTOGRAPHY

If a photograph is made by flash illumination alone, normal Zone System procedures can be applied if reflected light readings of the subject can be made. Many modern flash meters will read both incident and reflected light.

It requires at least one reflected low value reading and one high value reading. The exposure and development are figured by normal Zone System methods. There is a danger of reciprocity departure if the flash duration is very short and its effect on exposure and contrast must be considered.

Some flash meters are designed to make only incident readings of flash illumination and the problems encountered when using incident meters with the Zone System, apply. The flash meter in the incident mode will place a gray card of 18% reflectance on zone V. Other values must be estimated for Zone System placement or their reflectance values known.

When using the synchro-sun technique, either an incident or reflected meter can be used with equal efficiency.

Under controlled conditions (such as a studio) it is possible to measure the relative reflectance of objects compared to a gray card. The subject is measured under a constant light source and zone locations are determined by the subject's relationship to an 18% gray card in the same light.

For example, if an object measures two f-stops less than the gray card, it will be placed on zone III by the flash meter exposure; if it measures one stop more than a gray card, the incident meter's exposure will place it on zone VI. This can aid in certain studio photographs, and the conversion to zones is not difficult.

Synchro-Sun

When we combine flash illumination and natural light it is called synchro-sun photography. This term infers that we are synchronizing the two illumination types to make one photograph.

In Zone System use, synchro-sun techniques are usually applied in situations where the natural light must be supplemented and flash is used to illuminate low values because development controls are not possible or desirable. This assumption precludes special effects photography.

Many flash meters will measure flash and natural light *combinations* and these meters can be used to determine the amount of flash illumination that must be added for specific results. The procedure is simple and accurate.

Using a Flash Meter for Synchro-Sun Photography

1. Place the *high* value on the desired zone using a reflected light meter and normal zone placement techniques. Set the camera exposure to place the *high* value on the selected zone. Determine where the low zone falls on the zone scale.

2. Determine what zone you want the low value to be and note how many zones you must raise it for the desired result.

   For example, if we place the high value on zone VII and the low value measures five f-stops less, it falls on zone II. If we want the low value to be recorded as a zone III value, the exposure in that subject area must be increased one f-stop (one zone).

3. Set the meter to measure the natural light on the low zone value and note the recommended exposure. Then set the meter to measure the natural *and* flash illumination. Adjust the flash illumination to increase the exposure one full f-stop over the natural light reading for every zone you wish to raise it. Remember, the camera should be set to place the high value on the selected zone and only the flash illumination is changed. Be certain to set the meter at the shutter speed you will use to make the photograph so that it will take into account the correct natural light exposure.

If EV numbers are used (which I recommend), increase the exposure one EV for each zone you wish to raise the subject value.

For example, if the *natural light* exposure for the low value reads EV 10 and enough flash illumination is added to raise the *combination* reading to EV 11, the value has been raised one full zone. A combination reading of EV 12 would raise the value *two* full zones, etc.

The type of flash meter (incident or reflected) used to make the *combination* light readings is unimportant since we are only using it to measure how much flash illumination is *added* to the low value. The literal EV number that we read is also not important because we have already placed the low value by the exposure set on the camera. We only need to know how much we are *raising* the value.

Flash illumination may be adjusted by altering the power of the flash or changing the flash to subject distance. Covering the flash source with neutral density or diffusion is the easiest way to reduce light intensity and it eliminates the problems of working with the flash away from the camera.

Units of Light

If you do not have a flash meter it is necessary to convert the flash illumination into relative units of light to demonstrate how the flash illumination works. The notion of light units not only demonstrates how Zone System terminology can be used to express how the final gray tones in a print will look, but how "zones" are awkward in explaining certain technical concepts.

When we place a subject area on a zone we are exposing the film to a specific amount of light. It might be a very bright or very dark subject but it is still placed on a specific zone. All other objects in the scene expose the film according to their *relative* brightness.

Table A.2 expresses the relationship in light units of the exposure zones in a scene.

Because each zone requires twice as much light as the previous zone, the number of light units increases geometrically; it *doubles* each time. This shows that when a zone V value receives 16 *relative* units of light, a zone IV must receive 1/2 as much (8 units) and a zone III gets 1/4 as much light (4 units) because they are proportionately darker.

TABLE A.2

Zones	0	I	II	III	IV	V	VI	VII	VIII	IX
Light units	1/2	1	2	4	8	16	32	64	128	256

TABLE A.3

Zones	0	I	II	III	IV	V	VI	VII	VIII	IX
Pre-exposure units	2	2	2	2	2	2	2	2	2	2
Scene units	1/2	1	2	4	8	16	32	64	128	256
Total units	2 1/2	3	4	6	10	18	34	66	130	258

Pre-Exposure

The pre-exposure method demonstrates how light units are used. Exposing film to a single-toned subject, placed on zone II, gives the film 2 units of overall exposure. If we then expose the same film to a scene, it would have the scene exposure *plus* the 2 units from the first exposure. When we add the 2 units to the entire scene their effect can be predicted for each zone (see Table A.3).

The effect of the light units decreases in the higher zones because the percentage of total light is changed only slightly. The low zones are dramatically affected.

In the example, a zone II value is doubled but a zone VII value increases only a very small percentage. This reduces the difference between the zones and lessens the contrast of the negative. Note that the zone I value and the zone II value have moved much closer in total density to each other. The lowest density on the film is now 2 1/2 units. The contrast of the low zones is seriously reduced as well as the overall contrast of the negative.

Pre-exposures are usually made of even-toned, out-of-focus subjects like a clear sky or a gray card and this means that there is only density and *no image* recorded. It is a controlled fogging and affects the film by veiling the image. Pre-exposure must be kept to a minimum to avoid a severe loss of contrast in the low values. Pre-exposure placements of higher than zone III are not recommended.

Synchro-Sun Photography without a Flash Meter

A "correct" exposure when using the guide number for a flash will expose the film to the same relative units of light as exposing the film to natural light. That is, a value on zone V will be exposed to 16 *relative* units of flash illumination, a zone IV value will reflect 1/2 that amount (8 units) and so on, just as it would under a constant light source.

Since the main use of synchro-sun technique is to support low values without affecting the highs, the light being added by the flash must be low enough to affect only the low value we select.

Another way to think of this effect is to consider that if we use the exposure recommended by the guide number we *double* a zone V value in the scene. When we want to double a very low zone value we only need to give a small amount of extra light.

This is the same technique as the pre-exposure method even though the flash exposure and the natural light exposure are made at the same time. The flash need only be enough to raise the low value and not *all* of the values.

If we think of a flash guide number as always giving us a zone V exposure just like a light meter, it is always suggesting an f-stop that will put the same relative amount of light (16 units) into a scene because that is the correct number of units for a zone V exposure. The guide number works by trying to keep the *amount of light* added by the flash at a zone V exposure level. We are changing the placement of the subject values by altering the light source instead of using the f-stop or shutter speed.

Even if the concept of why this works is difficult, the actual use of light units is very simple.

When we use a guide number we are "placing" the *illumination level* (the intensity) of the light instead of placing subject areas. If we want to add a zone V illumination (16 units), we use the f-stop recommended by the guide number. If we only want the flash to add a zone IV light level (8 units), we must lower the added light level one f-stop from the guide number recommendation. Two f-stops less than the guide number recommendation, places the added illumination on zone III (4 units), etc. We add the number of light units we need by adjusting the flash illumination or the f-stop.

The reflectance of the subject is unimportant because when we place *any* zone value, then increase the light that illuminates that value, it will record as lighter even though its reflectance is the same. The *amount* of movement depends upon where the subject is originally placed because small amounts of added light may move a low value up a full zone while affecting a middle or high zone only minimally.

Procedure for Using Guide Numbers to Add Units of Light

1. Place the high value of the scene on the desired zone and note where the low value falls on the zone scale. Set this exposure on the camera. The number of units of light the low value receives from the natural light exposure can be read from Table A.2.
2. Determine how many zones the low value must be raised and the total number of light units that must be added to raise it to that zone.
3. Add the correct number of light units by adjusting the flash intensity, diffusing the source, changing the flash-to-subject distance or changing the f-stop.

That is, if the low value falls on zone II and we desire a zone III value (4 units total), we must add 2 units of light (2 + 2 = 4 units). We must reduce the guide number exposure by three f-stops because the guide number tells us how to make a zone V illumination level and we only want to add the equivalent of a zone II exposure (2 units).

We can adjust the flash intensity or use a smaller lens opening, but if the lens opening is changed, be certain to use the correct shutter speed to maintain the high value placement.

This procedure is not as hard as it sounds and the numbers may be confusing the first few times, but without a meter the flash exposure *must* be calculated manually. Alternate methods of using synchro-sun are effective, but they do not address the technique of moving a specific zone a specific amount. They deal with keeping light ratios within pre-determined limits and do not work well when combined with development changes. With practice and by using the same flash unit every time, the corrections become simple. An accurate guide number is essential.

Synchro-Sun Using an Incident Flash Meter Reading Flash Only

Meters reading flash only (incident meters) give an exposure recommendation similar to that calculated using the guide number for the flash unit. This exposure places the added illumination level on zone V by adding 16 relative units of illumination. Once the lens opening is read from the meter, it can be "placed" using the procedure detailed in the section on guide number use.

Considerations when Using Flash

While it is possible to provide some photographs with enough flash illumination to overcome severe contrast situations, I do not recommend it unless there is no alternative or the effect of artificial light is desired.

If adjusting the contrast range was the only consideration, any amount or type of supplementary flash would be acceptable. When not controlled carefully the flash becomes directional and its artificial nature is evident. Secondary highlights and even new shadows can be introduced if the flash intensity is too great or if its source is not diffused.

To maintain the basic character of the natural light, use the very minimum of additional illumination possible. If minus development is possible, use it for contrast reduction *before* resorting to flash. Try to *supplement* the normal Zone System methods, not replace them.

General Recommendations for Supplementing Natural Light

1. Apply normal Zone System controls as much as possible before resorting to additional illumination.
2. Use the minimum amount of flash needed for desired results.
3. The shadows in most natural scenes are lighted by a very diffuse combination of sky and environmental reflections. Generally, the more diffused the flash source, the more natural the effect.
4. To minimize secondary shadows and for the most natural effect, keep the flash source as close to the camera axis as possible.
5. While pre-exposure affects *all* low values in a scene, the flash effect on low values will change with the flash-to-subject distance.
6. The flash effect on *all* subject values must be considered. Moving a zone III value to a zone IV, causes *noticeable* changes in adjacent zone V values because the added illumination is high. Skin tones recorded in the zone V to VII range require fairly high flash illumination to change them and other high values in the scene may also be noticeably affected.

Scene										Film type		EI.	

Subject	Zones											Dev.
	0	I	II	III	IV	V	VI	VII	VIII	IX	X	

Filter

Bellows
$\dfrac{\text{Extension}^2}{\text{Focal length}^2}$ Adjustment for reciprocity effect

Base exposure

f-stop   Shutter speed

sec.   x   X   x   =   Total factor   x   Final exposure

Comments:

Scene										Film type		EI.	

Subject	Zones											Dev.
	0	I	II	III	IV	V	VI	VII	VIII	IX	X	

Filter

Bellows
$\dfrac{\text{Extension}^2}{\text{Focal length}^2}$ Adjustment for reciprocity effect

Base exposure

f-stop   Shutter speed

sec.   x   X   x   =   Total factor   x   Final exposure

Comments:

Sample exposure record for xeroxing by students.

BIBLIOGRAPHY

Adams, A., Basic Photo Series. Book 1, *Camera and Lens,* Revised ed. 1970. Book 2, *The Negative,* 1981. Book 3, *The Print,* 1968. Book 4, *Natural Light Photography.* Book 5, *Artificial Light Photography.* Superceded by The New Ansel Adams Photography Series. The New York Graphic Society, Boston, MA.

ANSI PH 2.2. 1981. American National Standard for Sensitometry for grading of black and white silver halide photographic papers for continuous tone reflection prints.

ANSI PH 2.5. 1979. American National Standard method for determining speed of photographic negative materials.

ANSI PH 3.49. 1971. (R1976). American National Standard for photoelectric type, general purpose, photographic exposure meters.

Carroll, B. H., G. C. Higgins, and T. H. James. 1980. *Introduction to Photographic Theory. The Silver Halide Process.* New York: John Wiley & Sons.

Davis, P. 1981. *Beyond The Zone System.* Somerville, Ma: Curtin & London, Inc., and New York: Van Nostrand Reinhold Co.

Dowdell, J. J. III, and R. D. Zakia. 1973. *Zone Systemizer for Creative Photographic Control.* Dobbs Ferry, NY: Morgan and Morgan, Inc.

Dunn, J. F., and G. L. Wakefield. 1981. *Exposure Manual,* 3rd. ed., Hartfordshire, England: Fountain Press.

Gassan, A. 1989. *Exploring Black and White Photography.* Dubuque, Ia: Wm. C. Brown Publishers.

Henry, R. J. 1988. *Controls in Black and White Photography.* Stoneham, Ma: Butterworth Pub.

Hirsch, R. 1989. *Color Photography.* Dubuque, Ia: Wm. C. Brown Publishers.

Johnson, C. 1986. *The Practical Zone System.* Stoneham, Ma: Butterworth Pub.

Lobel, L. and M. Dubois. 1987. *Basic Sensitometry,* 2nd. ed. London and NY: Focal Press.

Perrin, F. H. 1966. *The Theory of the Photographic Process,* 3rd ed. Edited by T. H. James. New York: The Macmillan Co.

Photolab Index, Dobbs Ferry, NY: Morgan & Morgan, Inc.

Picker, F. 1974. *Zone VI Workshop. The Fine Print in Black and White Photography.* Garden City, NY: AM Photographic Pub. Co., Inc.

Saltzer, J. 1979. *Zone System Calibration Manual.* Garden City, NY: Am Photographic Pub. Co., Inc.

Sanders, N. 1977. *Photographic Tone Control.* Dobbs Ferry, NY: Morgan & Morgan, Inc.

Schaeffer, J. P. 1983. *Zone System for Fine B & W Photography.* Tucson: H. P. Books.

Todd, H. N., and R. D. Zakia. 1969. *Photographic Sensitometry, The Study of Tone Reproduction.* Dobbs Ferry, NY: Morgan & Morgan, Inc.

Vestal, D. 1972. *The Craft of Black and White Photography.* New York: Harper & Row.

Wakefield, G. L. 1970. *Practical Sensitometry.* London: Fountain Press.

White, M. 1967. *Zone System Manual.* Dobbs Ferry, NY: Morgan & Morgan, Inc.

White, M. 1973. *The Visualization Manual.* Dobbs Ferry, NY: Morgan & Morgan, Inc.

White, M., R. Zakia, and P. Lorenz. 1976. *The New Zone System Manual.* Dobbs Ferry, NY: Morgan & Morgan, Inc.

INDEX